A PLUME BOOK

MY BOYFRIEND BARFED IN MY HANDBAG . . .
AND OTHER THINGS YOU CAN'T ASK MARTHA

JOLIE KERR is a Boston native and graduate of Barnard College, now residing in a teeny, tiny, spotless apartment in Manhattan's Lower East Side.

My Boyfriend Barfed in My Handbag...and Other Things You Can't Ask Martha

JOLIE KERR

A PLUME BOOK

PLUME
Published by the Penguin Group
Penguin Group (USA) LLC
375 Hudson Street
New York, New York 10014

USA | Canada | UK | Ireland | Australia
New Zealand | India | South Africa | China
penguin.com
A Penguin Random House Company

First published by Plume, a member of Penguin Group (USA) LLC, 2014

 REGISTERED TRADEMARK—MARCA REGISTRADA

LIBRARY OF CONGRESS CATALOGING-IN-PUBLICATION DATA
Kerr, Jolie.
My boyfriend barfed in my handbag . . . and other things you can't ask
Martha / Jolie Kerr.
pages cm
Includes index.
ISBN 978-0-14-219693-9
1. House cleaning. I. Title.
TX324.K48 2014
648'.5—dc23
2013022730

Printed in the United States of America
10 9 8 7 6 5 4 3 2 1

Set in Esprit

For Philip, and his Hair

Contents

Introduction

Oh, hey there and hello! If you're here it means that you've got a cleaning disaster on your hands. Or maybe it means that you've decided it's high time to learn how to keep your bedroom looking like it belongs to an adult, not a fourteen-year-old with a burning desire to assert your independence and irritate your mom with the power of stacks and stacks of clothes piled all about the place. Or maybe you, like me, just really, really love a gross story.

You've come to the right place.

In part, this is the right place because I know an awful lot about cleaning. I'm actually not entirely clear on how I got this way! I didn't go to Clean Person University or anything, and as far as I know there's no correspondence course one can take to learn how to mop a floor. I certainly don't come from one of those families where homekeeping is a skill passed down from generation to generation. My parents forced *The Double Helix* on me, not "Hints from Heloise."

I would have been happier with Heloise, had I been given that option.

I can't tell you exactly how I got this way, because it's a mystery on par with "Does God exist?" and "What *are* those Magic Erasers made of? Are they made of actual magic?" (melamine foam, actually). But I can tell you how it came to pass that I became a cleaning advice columnist, and I can also share a few stories that my friends told me when I asked them if they had any recollections of me as a clean person out in the wild. They did, it turned out. Do you want to hear those first? Sure you do.

I'm starting with this one from my friend Matt because you should know that my friends are wonderfully tolerant and also that wine factors prominently into our lives. I don't want you thinking it's all dish soap and no play for Jolie.

I usually serve you wine because I'm embarrassed to let you see the inside of my fridge and freezer. If you happen to open my fridge and/or freezer, you start pulling everything out and reorganizing the items in rows by size and frequency of use.

Who doesn't do that, I ask you? (In my defense, Matt was the man of honor at my wedding. We're *close*. It's not like I just wander into the homes of any old acquaintance and start reorganizing their foodstuffs.) I will, however, chide my pals if I feel they need it, as in the case of my dear friend Dan.

You (lovingly) shouted, "Launder your dish towels!" at me during the *Miss Advised* screening at my old apartment.

He needed to be told! I did so lovingly! (And wow, I guess now you know that we watch really, truly terrible reality programming.) Speaking of loving acts of cleaning kindness, how about this one?

> When I had serious sinus surgery, you cleaned my bathroom and kitchen from top to bottom while I was recovering! And you reassured me that if I bled on my sheets, we could tackle the stains with hydrogen peroxide! And then when I had to pull three feet of packing out of my face and I bled all over the bathroom, you cleaned it up so I wouldn't have to deal with the fact that enormous quantities of blood were pouring out of my nose and all over my white bathroom!

If you need me, I'll be shining my halo.

Speaking of my friends! It was another dear friend, Tyler Coates, who suggested to me that I ought to write a cleaning column. I thought he ought to round up a search party to go out looking for his mind, because he had clearly lost it. Fortunately, another friend, Edith Zimmerman, had just launched a new website, The Hairpin, and convinced me that Tyler's idea was a great one and that I should write that column for her site. Which I did, and that was how I got into the business of giving cleaning advice.

While writing the column, I learned a whole heap more about cleaning, which is what happens when confronted with what I truly hope are unique disasters, like a boyfriend who leaves skid marks on six-hundred-thread-count Pratesi sheets, in that I hope they never happen to someone else. And now you get to benefit from all the time I spent visiting places like StonerForums.com to find out the best way to clean up after spilling bong water all over a carpet, more car buff discussion boards than I could possibly count, and a site called Urge and Merge for tips on getting silicone lube stains out of sheets. Don't, by the way, visit Urge and Merge on your own. I'm a professional; leave that kind of dirty work to me.

In this book we'll cover some basics and some not-so-basics. Both of which will be fun, I promise! The basics will be fun because once we're done here, you'll never again have to sit despondently looking at your only good pan that you've ruined ("ruined"—you didn't ruin it! You just don't yet know how to save it. But stick with me, kid, I've got you covered on that.) or a mop that you don't know how to use (actually? Don't bother learning. Mops are nasty and we'll get into why and what the alternatives are). And, while it may not sound so fun now, it will be AWESOME the first time you have a disaster and realize that, "Wait a minute! I KNOW WHAT TO DO HERE! Oh my God, how did this happen?? THIS IS SO GREAT!"

As for the not-so-basics, well . . . hang on to your hats, and maybe also your lunch, because, oh yeah, we'll talk about barf. Barf on the walls, barf on the pillows, barf on your clothes, and, yes, barf in your handbag.

My Boyfriend Barfed in My Handbag . . . and Other Things You Can't Ask Martha

CHAPTER 1

The Kitchen: Clean It, or Just Set It on Fire and Be Done?

Raise your hand if you've ever seen a mouse scurrying through your kitchen.

Liars, every last one of you. Heck, even *I've* seen a mouse scurrying through my kitchen, and I'm a Clean Person. To be fair, it was a mouse of the field-ish variety, and my downstairs neighbors had just tilled the backyard in order to do their summer planting, and I'm pretty sure Fievel was running all about the place because his home had been disrupted. At least that's what I'm going to tell people, and if you don't toe the party line on this one, I won't tell you how to clean that burnt rice off the bottom of the only pan you own. So there!

Right, so let's talk kitchens: they're such great places—the heart of the home! But also? Woof, kitchens can get *gross*, can't they?? Grease splatters, spilled crumbs, overflowing garbage, the leaning tower of dishes in your sink—and those are the everyday problems, right? What about when mold engulfs your leftovers? (If that's an everyday problem for you, please don't tell me, okay? I don't know if my heart can take it.) Or when your freezer ices over such that it poses a realistic threat to the *Titanic*? Or when your husband decides to brew his own ginger beer and the glass growler he stored it in explodes from the pressure created by the fermentation process, leaving your kitchen covered in glass shards and sticky ginger beer? (This is a real thing that happened, by the way. The solution? Ammonia. And heavy-duty rubber gloves because ouch ouch be careful out there, that glass is pernicious!)

So now that you possess the very important knowledge of how to clean ginger beer from your cabinets, let's back it up a bit and cover some basics. Starting with how to hard clean a kitchen.

Or maybe I should start with an explanation of what I mean when I say "hard clean a kitchen"? Yes, let's start there.

In the industry, we differentiate forms of kitchen cleaning using the terms *daily clean*, *hard clean*, and *the full monty hard clean*. Okay that's a lie, there's no "industry" of people like me, and we don't have terms and conferences and such, but *oh, would that we did.* Anyway! Those are just the terms I use, and I like 'em, so I'm gonna keep 'em!

Right, so!

Daily Clean

These are, it will surprise you not to learn, the things you should do on a daily basis, allowing for adjustments if you're a person who doesn't use his or her kitchen every day. The basics are this:

- Wash the dishes
- Wipe down the counters

- Put all foodstuffs away and throw any garbage in the trash can
- Deal with any disasters as they happen

The idea is to establish a baseline of kitchen chores that allow the space to remain tidy and uninviting to critters and other pests. And, I mean, that's not too much, is it? You can wash a few dishes and give your counters a wiping without wanting to die from the crushing burden of it all, right??

That last bullet point, though . . . you'll want to know more about it, won't you? It is a truism that the longer you pretend that a mess doesn't exist, the harder it will be and the more time it will take to clean up. It's completely understandable to find yourself with a spilled container of leftovers in the fridge, or a pot of tomato sauce that boiled over onto your stove, and just say, "You know? To hell with this. I'm going to bed."

And while I'm generally a HUGE advocate of taking to one's bed when things go wrong, in the case of giant messes, I'd be remiss in my duties if I didn't tell you to allow yourself one minute in which you can huff and puff at yourself, the walls, the god who has clearly forsaken you, *who- or whatever*, but when that minute is up take a deep breath and just deal with the mess right then and there.

You'll be happy you did.

Hard Clean

The hard clean is the thing you'll want to do anywhere between once a week and once a month, depending on how you use your kitchen. And also, let's be honest, on your willingness to clean things. I'm giving timelines here because people like them, but I also want to make sure you know that really, this is a personal choice you can and should make for yourself. I'm not here to assign chores to you, just to suggest to you how and when to do things if you so desire such information.

One thing that the hard clean *is not* is a pantry-clearing operation. We'll get to that later on down the line. The hard clean is meant to address the kitchen grime that the daily clean doesn't—think greasy buildup on walls, splattered appliances, crumbs lurking in corners.

Step 1: Set aside 1–3 hours of your day!

Did you just do a double take? Yeah, I know. Sorry about that! But these things take time! However, the more often you clean, the less time it will take, which probably doesn't make you feel any better at all. What can I say, I tried.

The amount of time you'll need to make for this process is something you'll need to determine on your own. It will largely depend on the size of and relative filth situation in your kitchen. You'll also want to factor in the availability of helping hands. It bears mentioning that sometimes helping hands get in the way, so choose your helping hands wisely.

Step 2: Put on music!

The biggest mistake people make when setting out to tackle their chores is forgetting to put on music. It's basically the same theory behind listening to music at the gym: it gets you moving, perks you up, provides a rhythm to work along to. Cleaning is physical work! You will sweat! So, you know, treat big cleaning jobs just like you would a trip to the gym.

Unless you're a person who skips the trip to the gym, in which case please don't treat cleaning like a trip to the gym!

Step 3: Gather your arsenal!

The cleaning products you choose depend on a few factors: what you've got on hand, personal preference, the specific needs of your kitchen—for example, granite countertops are best cleaned using products that are different from what you'd use on butcher block—and what, if any, particular messes require your attention.

With that said, try to keep it simple with your products. Two, maybe three, cleansers should do it for you. Among those three you'll want an abrasive, a degreaser, and an all-purpose spray—preferably one that will shine up any metal; here, I'd highly recommend making your own solution of white vinegar and water. If you're more into brand-name items, Windex is great too. Specifically Windex. With apologies to the other brands of glass cleaner on the market, for my money Windex is so clearly (GET IT?? Sorry.) superior it's not even worth fussing about with another product. Unless it's white vinegar and water. Then you have my blessing to commit Windex adultery.

In terms of an abrasive, I use Soft Scrub, though not exclusively. Sometimes I go for Comet or Bon Ami; just understand that a powder abrasive cleaner is going to be more abrasive, and therefore more likely to scratch delicate surfaces, than is a cream abrasive cleaner. I have a deep and abiding hatred of Bar Keepers Friend, though many, many people love it so much they want to marry it, so I feel like I should mention it here. They make both a powder and a cream product. But seriously, I hate that stuff, and I know hate is a strong word BUT STILL. It's utterly irrational. (It's actually not *that* irrational; I've never had any success in using it to clean things it's often recommended for—stainless steel and enameled cast-iron cookware, both of which I collect and care for in the way normal people care for their children—and I'm an expert cleaner, so it sends me into a mad frenzy of not understanding why and how people are loving this stuff so much.)

My degreaser of choice is ammonia, mixed with water, which I use on the regular to wipe down the cabinetry, walls, the ventilation hood, my floors, young children with sticky fingers, etc. But that's just me! If you prefer a less toxic degreaser, try mixing Dawn dish soap with warm water and using that as your cleaning solution for greasy messes. But also, you're all grown adults with values and opinions and mothers who may have imparted upon you a devotion to certain products, and so by all means, you do you.

Once you've got all your products in hand, you'll need to assemble your accoutrements: A sponge, perhaps more than one. A few clean rags, swell things to have on hand. A roll of paper towels, yes, sure. BUT, BUT, BUT! Your hard clean should NOT be done with paper towels. First of all, it's foolishly wasteful, which is bad for our precious Mother Earth. But more important, paper towels will not cut it for the kind of cleaning we're talking about here. You'll want to have them nearby to do a final wipe-up, but you'll not want to rely on them to do the majority of your work.

If you choose to use something like bleach or ammonia that needs to be diluted into a solution, you'll also need a small bucket. You know what works really well for this and is kind of charming? Those plastic beach pails we all had as kids—why not add some fun and whimsy to your cleaning routine? The other nice thing about them is that they have a handle, so you can carry your washing solution around the kitchen easily as you move from space to space.

Last but absolutely not least, you'll need a pair of rubber gloves to protect your hands, Miss Scarlett!

Step 4: Clear all the things out!

All of them. Every last thing on your countertops must be moved to a secure location. Clearing everything out includes washing, drying, and putting away any dirty dishes in the sink. Now, listen, I know you, and I know you're going to try to cheat and (1) I'll know and (2) you'll only end up making more work for yourself down the road if you skimp on this step. I really promise that something that will take so much less time than you think will save you so much energy and annoyance and extra work in the next stages, so just do it.

But actually here, you have a decision: does your situation call for just a surface clean, or do you require a full-on pantry purge? Probably for most of you the surface clean will suffice. We'll get to the pantry purge when we tackle the full monty hard clean.

Step 5: Take a break!

I'll let you in on a secret: the hardest part is over. More or less, from here you're going to coast, and that's because you took the time to prepare. Bet you didn't see this coming, eh? So as a reward for your hard work, would you care for a cold beer or soda? I bet you would. Remember to buy some before you start this project. You'll get to make the best shopping list! It'll be like:

- Soft Scrub
- Sponges
- Beer
- Paper towels

Step 6: CLEAN!

A HUGE rule of cleaning is to always work top to bottom. If
you do your floors first and then wipe off a counter full of
crumbs, guess where those crumbs are going? Yeah, right
on your clean floor that's no longer clean and will need to be
redone. So! Start from the top and work downward. Wipe the
cabinetry, then the walls and backsplashes, then the countertops, then the appliances (refrigerator, stove, microwave,
etc.), ending with the floors. Because cabinet and countertop
materials vary so greatly from kitchen to kitchen, a bit later
in the chapter we'll go over the particulars of which products
should be used on which cabinet and counter types. Stay
tuned for a handy chart!

Leave the sink be until the very, very end of the process;
the sink will serve as your home base for dumping out dirty
wash water, rinsing and wringing out sponges and rags, and
probably some other gross things that we don't really need to
talk about. (Dead bugs. I'm talking about dead bugs, you
guys.)

If you're feeling really brave, you might even take a look-
see at the top of your cabinets. You may discover that they
are wearing a dirt sweater! I might have learned this the
hard way! Prepare to be so, so, so, so, so grossed out!

Step 7: Put all the things back!

You're so close to done! Which means it's time to gather up
all the things you removed to a secure location and return
them to their homes. But before you do so, please consider
grabbing your trash can to execute a merciless decluttering.
Most normal people have a ton of junk that they don't need
taking up space in their kitchens—and collecting filth! Old

twist ties, unopened mail, mementos from three relation-
ships ago that you're holding on to because you have an utter
inability to admit when something is truly over, even though
you're the one who ended it and frankly you've never regret-
ted a thing except that that ceramic lighthouse that you
bought together on a trip to Maine is really just so special
to you.

Put that ceramic lighthouse in the trash.

Once you've thrown away anything you don't need, take
a gander at what's going back into your squeaky-clean
kitchen. Are things sticky or dusty or greasy or some combination of all three? Wipe them down. A damp rag should
suffice, you probably don't even need a product, but if you do
that's where all-purpose cleaner comes in handy. Later on,
we'll go through the care and keeping of small appliances,
like toasters and coffeepots, so stay with me for that.

Step 8: Clean up after yourself!

"But I've just cleaned for hours!" Which is true, and I'd like
to take a moment to tell you that you did a great job! Hurrah
for you! But you also created a little bit of a mess in that process, so: dump out the dirty washing water and rinse out
your bucket, then rinse and wring out your sponges and
rags. Put the cleaning products away. Throw paper towels in
the trash, and tie up the bag and take it out if it's full.

Last but not least: clean the sink with an all-purpose
spray and a sponge; you can also use a product for stainless
steel or porcelain if that's what your sink is made of. The
important thing is to rid it of the dirt and grime that accumulated when you rinsed rags and dumped out cleaning.

Actually, wait, no, that's not the last step, *this* is the last step:
take a good look at your whole kitchen. Admire your work! Isn't

it amazing?? It's okay if you want to lick the countertops; we can give you two a minute alone to get intimate with each other.

Speaking of your countertops, remember how I promised you a handy chart explaining how to clean all manner of kitchen cabinet and countertop materials? Well, here it is!

Countertop/ Cabinet Type	Products to Use	Products to Avoid	Cleaning Method
Butcher Block	White vinegar; liquid dish soap	Too much water, which can cause splitting or warping	Apply the vinegar or soap to a damp sponge or soft cloth; wipe counters with the grain; dry thoroughly
Stainless Steel	White vinegar; liquid dish soap	Ammonia; bleach; abrasive cleansers and/or brushes	Wipe the counters in a straight line; blot dry with a soft cloth to prevent streaking
Tile	Liquid dish soap; all-purpose cleaner; OxiClean; rubbing alcohol	Oil-based soaps; ammonia	Wipe tile down in a circular motion; use a soft-bristled toothbrush to clean grout if necessary
Formica	All-purpose cleaner	Abrasive cleaners and/or brushes	Spray all-purpose cleaner on a soft rag and wipe counters; rinse with a clean, wet sponge or rag
Linoleum	All-purpose cleaner	Ammonia	Spray all-purpose cleaner on a soft rag and wipe counters; dry with a soft cloth
Granite	Stone soap; mild liquid dish soap and warm water	Products containing lemon, vinegar, or other acids; scouring powders or creams	Wash with a sponge or soft cloth; rinse thoroughly so as to avoid soap buildup; dry completely with a soft cloth

Marble	Stone soap; mild liquid dish soap and warm water	Products containing lemon, vinegar, or other acids; scouring powders or creams; rust removers	Wash with a sponge or soft cloth; rinse thoroughly so as to avoid soap buildup; dry completely with a soft cloth

The Full Monty Hard Clean

This is the hard clean that addresses the innards of your kitchen in addition to the exterior surfaces that we addressed in the regular hard clean. You can treat these as one task or two separate projects. If your kitchen is huge and you have a vast pantry, I hate you. Oh, and also you'll probably benefit from treating a cabinet/pantry cleanup as a thing you do apart from tackling the counters, appliances, sink, etc. It will save your sanity, and you'll also be much more likely to complete the task if you take it on in that manner. If your kitchen and storage space are tiny, come sit by me and we'll weep over it together.

The instructions for a pantry clean are actually really simple, which is deceptive. It's simple, but it is most assuredly time-consuming, and far more frustrating than you'd expect. This is true for two main reasons: (1) the pantry has a lot more stuff in it than you'd think and (2) it requires that you throw things away, which can be agonizing for a lot of people. It feels wasteful! I'll offer this by way of advice: if something in your pantry isn't being used, it's no more wasteful sitting there than it will be in your trash.

Real talk.

Just like with the regular hard clean, the first step is to take everything out of the pantry or cabinet. If you're working with multiple cabinets, consider tackling one or two at a time based on what's stored in them. If you've got no discernible order to how you've stored things, then take everything out all at once, because you should take this opportunity to make sense of things. Your life will be much easier if you're storing all your glasses together rather than jumbling them in with your dried bean and bouillon collection.

Once everything is out of the way, it's time to clean all the interior surfaces. If there are a lot of crumbs and you've got one, a handheld vacuum cleaner is a good first pass. Then, using a sponge or a rag—but not paper towels because they're not tough enough for this—wipe down the shelves, back, and sides of the cabinets. Good old soap and water is great for this! Just, like, the dish soap you've already got hanging around in your kitchen space. But if you feel you want or need something stronger, you can use an all-purpose cleaner.

If you find that you have sticky spills to contend with— honey is a common offender—grab a rag and soak it in hot water, as hot as you can stand. Wring it out and press it on the honey; the hot water will liquefy it, rendering it easier to wipe up. If there are greasy spills, such as oil, ammonia is the ticket. Just be sure that you're not using another product that contains bleach, as bleach + ammonia = sudden death. Okay, not really sudden death, but the two in concert produce a lethal gas, and that is no joke. You'll hear me bang on about this again because it's a super important cleaning lesson to learn: NEVER MIX BLEACH WITH AMMONIA. It will kill you. And then you'll be dead, and your house won't be clean, and people will judge you, THE END.

Once the cabinets are clean, leave the doors open to allow them to dry while you turn your attention to the stuff you've taken out.

Get out your garbage pail, take a deep breath and prepare to purge, purge, purge. Check expiration dates and throw away anything past its prime. Toss out things you don't use and/or donate any unopened dry or canned goods. Try to find the joy in this—it's really very freeing! If you start to get the agita over the amount of things you're getting rid of, that are going to waste, remind yourself of my earlier advice: if you're not using it, it's no more wasteful in the trash can than it is in your pantry.

Then you'll want to survey what's left and begin grouping things. Do this *before* you begin putting things away, because the size of your groupings will help you to determine where best to place them. Then, once like things are with like things, go ahead and restock your shelves. Put bulky and less-often-used items on higher shelves and the things you reach for most often in the most convenient spot. If you've got a lot of small, loose items like tea bags or sugar packets, put them in a small container to keep them from roaming about willy-nilly. If you have open bags of staples like flour and sugar, consider investing in glass or plastic storage containers to help prevent spillage. Or worse.

Which brings us to this: unfortunately, one of the circumstances under which you might find yourself needing to execute a hard clean and/or a full monty hard clean on your kitchen is if you have a critter invasion. So let's talk a bit about what to do if uninvited guests of the pestilent variety make their way into your home.

First of all—and this is so important to me—I don't want you to get upset with yourself if it happens. Unless you really and truly are leaving foodstuffs and garbage strewn all over the house, you didn't bring this upon yourself. Vermin and insects happen. Especially in urban areas and/or in warmer months when we often have our windows open. But—and this is equally important to me—you've really got to get right on top of things as soon as possible. The instinct to flee or pretend like nothing is wrong is one that you must fight, fight, fight. And when you're done fighting that, you'll get right into fighting off the invaders. Like you're a Viking or something. Just think of it that way. You have my permission to wear one of those plastic horned Viking helmets if it will make you feel better about things.

Given the pesty nature of critters, it should come as no surprise to learn that different sorts of bugs and vermin require different elimination strategies. So we'll take them by type and then scream and pull at our hair and then pour a stiff drink because shudderrrrrrr.

Critter	Character Traits	What He Loves	What He Hates
Pantry Moth	• Brown, winged creatures • Insidious things	• Grains • Plastic, cardboard, and foil containers/wrappers that he can chew through	• Cupboard moth traps • Bay leaves • Essential oils such as peppermint, eucalyptus, tea tree, or citronella • Glass or metal containers
Fruit Fly	• Winged • Reproductively blessed • Not very smart • Cannot swim	• Fruit • Wine • Beer • Apple-cider vinegar	• Wine, beer, apple-cider vinegar, or fruit juice in a jar or high-sided bowl with a few drops of dish soap. Fruit flies are attracted to the liquid and fly into the trap. The dish soap coats their wings, rendering them unable to fly out to safety, and they will drown. That got kind of sad.

Ant	• Lives in colonies • Sends out scouts to check out your home—beware the lone ant! • Enjoys marching, particularly two by two	• Sugar • Greasy foods/ residue	• Ant baits • Ant insecticide aerosols • Boric acid • Pepper • Cinnamon • Peppermint • Salt • Bay leaves
Cockroach	• Night owls • Reproductively blessed • Disease and bacteria carriers • Vile, pestilent things • Prone to skittering	• Coffee • Water • All foodstuffs	• Roach Motels • Boric acid* • Bay leaves *When using boric acid, less is more, as roaches and other critters will walk around it if the powder is piled too high. A thin lining of boric acid along baseboards and such will suffice!*
Silverfish	• Silvery, a half inch long • Night owls	• Dark, wet places • Starchy foods • Sugar • Wallpaper paste • Books, paper, and natural fibers • Mold and fungus	• CimeXa Insecticide Dust • D-Fense Dust • Intice Granular Bait • Dekko Silverfish Paks

Critter	Character Traits	What He Loves	What He Hates
Centipede	• Leggy • Fast-moving	• Moist environments • Clutter • The dark • Bedbugs, silverfish, spiders, termites, roaches—centipedes eat 'em!	• Aerosol insecticides • Sticky traps • The bottom of your shoe
Spider	• Hangs out in a web • Leggy	• Other insects	• Diatomaceous earth • Eucalyptus • The bottom of your shoe
Mouse	• Scurrying, furry, beady-eyed hell demons	• Your food supply • Warmth	• Glue traps • Mouse poison • Peppermint oil and mint leaves • Ammonia • Cats

I think I'm going to stop here. You probably already have. That's so sad; there's still so much book to read! So, hey, how about we talk about something more fun? Like doing your dishes? Wait, what's that? You don't think that's at all fun? Mmm-hmm, we'll see about that.

Your Sinks and Dishes

I can hear you now. Here's what you sound like, *Holy crap, this lady* still *has more to say about cleaning kitchens?? I'm exhausted just* reading *this, how can I be expected to actually* do *this stuff when I'm in such a state??*

I mean, I know, I'm exhausted too, but I can't let you leave without explaining to you how to do your darn dishes. Take, for instance, this poor woman.

Dishes 101

I just moved to a new place with a not-tiny, not-galley kitchen—hooray! But there are some issues: Firstly, I have been so spoiled, as this is the first place I've ever lived without a dishwasher (I know!). Could you maybe do a Dishes 101 thing? Like, I put them in the sink and wash them every day or two, but I always seem to make a mess because as soon as I turn on the water, it splashes off all of the dishes in the sink and onto me. There's no counter space next to the sink not taken up by my dish drainer, and putting dirty dishes on the counter behind me, then transferring them to the sink one by one doesn't seem any less messy. Also, my drying rack looks big when it's empty, but somehow it only seems to fit five dishes max after I wash them. I admit that my sense of spatial reasoning is not great—what am I doing wrong here?

While it's not a straight one-to-one, I think telling you about the method I use when I move into a new place and need to get all my dish- and silverware cleaned after unpacking them might be enlightening for you: Plug the drain, place all the items in the bottom of the sink, squirt the whole mess down with dish soap, and run the hot water until the sink is about two inches from overflowing. Then walk away.

Ten or so minutes later, hustle on back! What you're going to do is to dive in with your sponge and wash all of the items while they're still submerged in the soapy water; this will help with your splashing problem. While you wash, you might want to create a dirty side and a clean side to help keep things straight.

Once everything has been scrubbed, drain the sink completely and begin the process of rinsing each item. Give everything a look-see to make sure you've gotten them fully clean, going back over any stuck-on food with your sponge if need be.

To help with your drying-rack issue, try rinsing like things together, i.e., first rinse the plates, then the bowls, then the cutlery, and so on. That way, you'll be able to maximize the space in your drying rack by placing similarly shaped and sized items together. You can also stop at a sensible point in the rinsing cycle, turn off the water and towel dry the items in the drying rack and put them back in the cupboards. It probably sounds like *such a pain* to do that, but actually you'll find it's not that disruptive to switch tasks about halfway through the process, especially because it gives your hands a little break from the harsh realities of the washing water.

A couple more tips:

- Set aside knives and other sharp utensils so that you don't plunge your hand into the soapy water and impale yourself. Wash those separately.
- Use Palmolive dish soap. I've tried other brands and frankly none have the sudsing or staying power of Palmolive. Though I will admit that Mrs. Meyer's, while pricey, is delicious smelling and gives pretty good suds.
- Replace your sponges regularly. One of my college roommates had the most curious litmus test to determine whether a sponge was ready to be tossed: would you put your tongue on it? Isn't that so gross to think

about but also an interesting point?? If you want to extend the life of a grungy sponge, you can sanitize it by wetting it and then microwaving it for one to two minutes on a high setting.

- For those who have space for it, lay a dish towel (or two, depending on how many dishes you've got) out on the counter next to the sink to place larger or awkwardly shaped items to air-dry.

- Figure out how many dish towels you need and then buy double that number.

Burnt and/or Stuck-on Gunk

Scorching a favorite pot is a terrible thing to have happen. It's even a terrible thing to have happen when it's *not* your favorite pot that's been scorched. HOWEVER! I come bearing fantastic news: there's a super easy solution to it: Sprinkle baking soda allllllll over the bottom of the scorched pot and fill it about a third of the way up with water. Set the pot on your stovetop over a medium-high flame and let the water–baking soda solution come to a boil. Remove the pot from the heat, place it in the sink until it's cool enough to handle, and wash with a soapy sponge. The scorch marks should slide right off. *Et voilà!* A shiny pot, just waiting for its next big job.

Dishwashers

But what of those people who are lucky enough to *have* a dishwasher? We should beat them with reeds, yes. But when we're done with that, maybe we can be nice and help them out when they have smell issues.

If your dishwasher has developed a funk, there's a pretty simple solution: fill the bottom of the washer with about a half gallon of white vinegar and then run the machine while it's empty. You can and should also check to make sure there are no food chunks or buildup caught in the bottom of the machine (you can roll the bottom drawer out to get a better look at what might be lurking underneath). If you hate the smell of white vinegar or just feel like throwing your money at a more professional-sounding product, there's also something called Dishwasher Magic that you could totally check out.

Garbage Disposals

Ugh, God, a grotty garbage disposal, ugh, God, GROTTY!! The thing that often happens with garbage disposals is that food particles collect themselves on the walls of the disposal, creating an awful stench. Citrus peel as freshener is a great trick—basically, you just want to toss half a lemon/lime/ orange/grapefruit down the disposal, let 'er rip, and allow the grinding action to pull out all those fabulous smelling oils the fruits are holding up in their skins—but not one that's going to really get things clean. If you've got a smell problem that a grinding of the citrus won't touch, the thing that you'll want to do is plug the drain and fill the sink half-to-three-quarters of the way up with cold water and dishwashing soap—you could also use OxiClean, white vinegar, castile soap, baking soda, or bleach. Then you'll pull the plug and turn on the disposal. When the water level in the sink starts to get low, turn the cold water on and let the thing run for a minute or two. This will create a terrible racket. Maybe buy earplugs?

Which leads me to this approach, that I could never actually handle because I have the hearing of a bat and MY GOD WHAT IS THAT NOISE???: throw a dozen or so ice cubes down the drain, sprinkle rock salt over the cubes, and then flip the switch on the disposal, letting it run until the ice is completely ground. But seriously, WHAT IS THAT NOISE?

Plastic Cutting Boards and Food Storage Containers

If you find yourself with stained plastic cutting boards and/or plastic storage containers, a thick paste of baking soda and water applied with a sponge will help to eradicate the unsightly discoloration. Which is great, since just about everyone has baking soda in their kitchen. There are other things you can do—use a denture tablet dissolved in hot water; fill the container with water, add a half teaspoon of bleach to it, and let it soak—but they're not nearly as convenient as the baking soda approach.

But what of the place where you keep all the things you cut up on that cutting board and put in those storage containers?? Yes, the refrigerator, hurrah for the refrigerator, except ooooh eeeewww how long has that been in there? Actually, never mind, I don't want to know.

How to Hard Clean a Refrigerator

There are really only two things you need to know about hard cleaning a fridge: what cleaning product(s) to use and the importance of taking everything out of the unit before you begin. The reason for imparting the latter piece of knowledge to you is that you won't truly be able to get your icebox clean unless you can get at every surface and also that part of hard cleaning a fridge is getting rid of old, expired, or unwanted foodstuffs. It's also helpful to take everything out so you can survey what you have duplicates of and stop buying those things at the market until you've run through your current stash.

In terms of your products, this is a place where white vinegar is your best bet. It's a fantastic cleaner, and also nontoxic, so you won't run the risk of having any leftover chemical residue hanging out alongside the delicious lasagna you made last night. For wiping, you'll want a combination of a sponge or rag *and* paper towels. Both. Not just one or the other—both. Because refrigerators often house sticky spills and splatters and God only knows what else. I'd give Dobie pads a STRONG BUY rating—they're sponges covered in a nylon netting, which will help you to scuff things off the walls without damaging the plastic with scratches and dings.

Now that you've got your tools and have agreed with me about the importance of taking everything out, go ahead and empty the contents of the unit. Have a trash bag or garbage pail nearby and throw away anything suspect before you even start cleaning. If you have foodstuffs covered in plastic wrap or tinfoil, use it to protect your hand while you scoop old food into the trash can—that's a personal favorite from my stash of little tricks that I'm sharing for those of you who have tactile issues with handling old food (and who doesn't, really?). Alternatively: wear rubber gloves. Set items you're keeping on the countertops and/or in a cooler.

Once everything is out, remove the shelves and drawers and wash them with hot soapy water in the sink or tub. I find that the tub is better for this because it gives you more room to wash those kind of awkwardly shaped items, which means less sudsy water all over the place. The other advantage of using the tub is that it frees up the sink, allowing you to fill it with hot soapy water and put any storage containers, pots, pans, jars, other things I probably don't want to know about, pitchers, etc., that you've taken out and emptied of their contents right in to soak. Of course, if you don't have a tub on the same floor as your kitchen, this might be a pain. If you don't have a tub at all, this might be an impossibility.

With everything out of the unit, it's time to turn your attention to getting the interior of the fridge looking great. This is also the easiest and most satisfying part! Spray the walls, ceiling, and floor of the fridge with white vinegar solution, wipe 'em down with your Dobie pad, wipe the whole thing out with dry paper towels, and that's sort of it. If there are major stains, a Magic Eraser will help. One thing worth noting is that depending on how gross things are, this process might take some elbow grease, so don't be surprised if these easy-sounding instructions end up being more work than you anticipated.

Now you're ready to put the racks and shelves and drawers back in place and then comes the really, really, really fun part: putting alllllll the foodstuffs back in and organizing them! Wheee! SUCH FUN!!!!!

Tips on Organizing a Refrigerator

First you'll want to survey what you've got and group things together. You should have taken a first pass at pitching old, expired, or unwanted items when you took everything out, but do a second pass now just to be sure.

Then, before things go back in, wipe down sticky bottles,

tighten lids, snap Tupperware tops back in place, tell your
favorite jar of mustard how nice that tie looks on him. Remind your things that they're special. Then put everything
back in a way that makes sense to you. Some ideas:

- Keep labels facing out so you can easily distinguish
  similar-looking items from one another.
- Put things you don't use often toward the back of the
  unit.
- Put taller items behind shorter ones so it's easier to see
  what you've got in there.
- Make a note of things you have duplicates of and stop
  buying those things, you crazy jam hoarder.
- Put raw meat and eggs on the bottom shelf so if there's
  a leak it doesn't contaminate your other food.
- Don't store temperature-sensitive items like milk in the
  door of the unit.
- Every time you take out your trash, open your refrigerator before tying up the bag and throw away any old
  food.

Okay, now look at where your things are. From now on,
that's where those things go. When you come home from the
grocery store, the milk should go in the same place it was
before. This sounds a little much! And at first you're going to
be annoyed with me for making you do this. But doing so
will create a habit that helps to keep you organized, and
within a few weeks it will be second nature for you to always
put the milk where it belongs, and then you'll turn into the
sort of person who wants to throttle your roommate for putting the Crystal Light pitcher in the wrong place.

Defrosting and Cleaning a Freezer

Defrosting a freezer is, truth be told, a wreck of a process. If you find yourself needing to defrost your freezer, go ahead and couple it with hard cleaning your fridge, since you'll need to remove everything anyway. Also do the defrosting first, then the cleaning. It's grim business, I'm telling you.

To start, you'll need to take everything out of the freezer *and* the refrigerator and put frozen and/or perishable items in a cooler. (You can get an inexpensive cooler at any major chain drugstore; depending on how much stuff you have, you might need two, but also you should treat this as a good opportunity to throw away old or expired foods.) Now unplug the unit.

Line the bottom of the refrigerator with old towels or T-shirts or rags to absorb the water as the freezer defrosts and things head south. Depending on the configuration of the unit, you may need to put a towel down in the freezer as well. You might also want to put a garbage bag down on the floor in front of the fridge to catch any water that runs out, so your floors don't get damaged. The plastic bag is also useful for when it's time to gather up the sopping wet towels used to absorb the melted ice.

Now we wait.

Once the defrosting is complete, take those wet towels out of the refrigerator and then go over the interior of both the fridge and freezer with a dry towel. Then spray the interior of both spaces with white vinegar and water solution and wipe everything down. Now you can put your things away and lie down.

Keep a Freezer Frost-Free

If things start getting a little icy in your freezer, you should think about doing some spot-defrosting, which will help prevent the freezer from achieving a *Titanic*-level iceberg state that requires a full defrosting, which is a mess and to be avoided at all costs.

Fill a large pot with water and bring it up to a rolling boil; while you're waiting for it to boil, remove everything from the freezer and, if you've got one, put it all in a cooler. If you don't have a cooler, you can store frozen goods in the refrigerator for the duration of this process.

Pour some of the boiling water into a bowl that will fit inside your freezer (you'll want to check this first), put it in, and close the door. Switch the water out for fresh boiling water a few times—it will take a little while for it to work, but the ice will defrost eventually.

Another option is to turn your hair dryer up to the highest setting it can go and point it at the icicles. I've tried this and found it to be too frustratingly slow for big jobs, but it works nicely on smaller floes.

At the risk of insulting your intelligence, it also bears suggesting that you may want to turn up the freezer temperature so things don't ice over as much.

USING FOODSTUFFS TO SOLVE YOUR CLEANING CONUNDRUMS

One of the more enjoyable parts of my job is the reaction I get when I tell people about all the weird and wonderful uses for foodstuffs when it comes to cleaning. Many people know about the efficacy of vinegar or baking soda or lemon when it comes to cleaning, but how about salt? Or Tabasco sauce? Gotcha! Now you're hooked.

Product	Use For
Cornstarch	Removing oil and grease stains from clothes, especially delicate fabrics
Cornmeal	Use to pull oil and dirt out of faux or real fur linings on coats, boots, and so on
Baking Soda	Sprinkle liberally into scorched cookware, cover with boiling water, let sit until cool, and then wipe out—it will remove any burnt-on gunk; combine with vinegar to get vases and other oddly shaped items clean; make a paste and apply to food that's stuck onto a range top or in an oven; use in laundry for fresher-smelling clothes
Sliced Bread	Picking up shattered glass shards
Potatoes	Cut in half and use the cut side to pick up shattered glass shards
Ketchup	Polishing brass and copper
Tabasco	Polishing copper
White Wine	Removes red wine stains
Club Soda	Removes red wine and other dark stains (especially helpful to know when out at a bar, restaurant, or party!)
Olive Oil	Rehydrates dried-out wood, such as chopping boards
Table or Sea Salt	Mix with water and use as an abrasive scrubber (sea salt); absorbs red wine stains
Lemon	Freshen up a stinking garbage disposal; cleaning a microwave; removing rust stains
Vodka	Eliminates odors
White Vinegar	Everything. Seriously. Have you been paying attention?

Ovens

Ovens should be cleaned as needed, which is a tricky thing to determine because some folks use theirs every day and others use theirs to store their shoes. Also, those people should stop doing that unless they want charred Manolos. Because I promise you, one day someone will turn your shoe oven on, and I'm not even going to entertain your crying when that happens. (Okay, fine, of course I will—I'm a total softie. But I'll definitely say, "I told you so!")

Using Oven Cleaner

Cleaning an oven using oven cleaner is one of those terrifying tasks that one is likely to avoid altogether because normal people fear death and there's something about the notion of spraying noxious chemicals in a place where there is gas or electricity or both that leads most rational folks to think to themselves, "No. No no no. Nope! Too scary."

However, cleaning an oven using oven cleaner is a good thing to know how to do, even for people who have self-cleaning ovens. Oh, right, and in terms of instructions on how to use your self-cleaning oven, your manufacturer's guide will tell you the things you need to know. Different models have different instructions, so you should follow the ones for your specific model rather than, say, those for your best friend's Viking.

Right, then, and back to our oven cleaner lesson. To take away some of the terror, go with Easy-Off oven cleaner, which is used on a cold oven. Somehow a cold oven filled with chemicals is much less terrifying than a hot one filled with chemicals, wouldn't you agree?

The thing is though . . . IT STINKS. Even the odor-free

kind. So open as many windows as you can while you're working with this product. And you absolutely must—no ifs, ands, or buts about it—use rubber gloves when working with it. You will not have hands left to cook with if you forgo the rubber gloves.

With all of that out of the way, here are your instructions, broken out into steps so you'll know exactly what you're getting into before you begin.

Step 1: Spray the entire interior of the oven with the cleaner—walls, floor, roof, door, as well as the racks. Now shut the oven door and consider leaving the room, because ooooh boy, are things ever going to start smelling. After ten minutes, return to your kitchen, take in the *lovely* smell, and gird your loins because this next part is going to suck.

Step 2: Fill a bucket with clean water, grab a sponge with a scrubber side to it, and put on your rubber gloves. Open the oven and remove the racks; put them in the sink. Close the oven door to try to keep some of the chemical stench at bay, maybe? Using a wet sponge, wipe down the racks, rinsing them with water when you're done and setting them aside to drip-dry.

Step 3: Plop down on the floor in front of the oven, wet the sponge, and wring it out, and then begin wiping each surface, starting with the side walls. There may be some tricky spots—turn your sponge and use the scrubber side to get at them. Once the sides are done, do your best Sylvia Plath impersonation and stick your head all the way in the oven; once you're in there, wipe down the back wall, then the roof of the oven, saving the oven floor for last. The reason you want to do the floor of the oven last is that all the muck and cleaner from the sides, back, and ceiling will fall onto the oven floor while you're cleaning them, so do remember to work top-down.

Throughout this process, you'll need to rinse your sponge frequently; you will also probably need to change the water halfway through. Given this, it's important to wash the oven racks first so you can remove them from the sink to dry, leaving that space open for you to dump the dirty wash water and refill your bucket.

Step 4: When the oven is clean and mostly free of any oven cleaner residue, go in with damp paper towels or a clean sponge and give it one last going-over to ensure that it's been completely wiped out. Then replace the racks, close the oven, and pour a stiff drink, because Lordy, that was hell.

In closing: this is a disgusting, dirty job. Of all the chores in this book, this is certainly one of the grossest and most unpleasant. But it's also insanely satisfying to admire the oven when you're done, so you've got that to look forward to.

Making a Stovetop Gleam

Now that you've taken on the absolutely disgusting job of cleaning the oven, how about tackling the relatively easy task of getting your stovetop looking spiffy?

Most modern stovetops are made of either enamel (the painted-looking ones), or glass (the ones with the flat heating coils) or stainless steel (the metal ones), the cleaning method for each of which we'll take on separately.

Enamel

Remove the burners to the sink; soak them in hot soapy water while you work on the surface of the stove. Using a sponge, wet down the stove fairly well—I find that soaking the sponge and sort of wringing it over the range while keeping the sponge moving works best for this—and sprinkle a mild abrasive cleanser like Bon Ami all over the place. Then get after it with your wet sponge, scrubbing a little hard at any cooked-on gunk. Rinse the sponge well and wipe away all the excess cleanser; if there's any greasy residue, put a small amount of dish soap on the sponge and wipe the surface down to remove it before wiping clean. The last thing to do to really make the stovetop sparkle is to go over it with a dry paper towel or rag, which will pick up any lint or dust and eliminate streaks that the moisture may have left behind.

If you've got really bad stuck-on food that an abrasive cleanser won't get up, try sprinkling baking soda all over the whole mess and then spritzing it with white vinegar. You'll get a fun eruption of foam and hissing, which is always good for a thrill! Let it sit for about fifteen minutes and then wipe it up. You may need to do more than one application, depending on how bad things are, but eventually it will cut through the mess. And actually, it's worth noting that the baking soda and vinegar method will work on all three common stovetop surface types.

Glass and Stainless Steel

Use a white vinegar solution or glass cleaner to wipe the surface. If burnt-on food is an issue, put some baking soda on a wet sponge and scrub the stovetop. There are also good products specifically for cleaning glass or stainless steel stovetops, which you should check out if you want—but vinegar and or baking soda is cheaper. Entirely up to you, though! One thing to note is that you shouldn't use anything harsher than baking soda on glass or stainless, as it will scratch. A dry cloth will also go a long way to prevent streaking on both surfaces.

Cleaning a Greasy Vent Hood

The hood over your stove just loves to trap grease, and then that grease likes to attract dust, and before you know it there's some kind of new fabric manufacturing itself above your stove. Which would be great if you were in the business of inventing and manufacturing new types of fabric, but you are likely not actually in that business, in which case why are you growing fabrics in your kitchen? Stop that, maybe.

Still, though, your fabric-growing kitchen-farm is probably not nearly as gross as this poor lady's kitchen.

NASA, We Have a Grease Problem

This is seriously gross: I was making pasta, and this HUGE DROP OF GREASE fell from the filter vent above the stove, directly into the pasta water, and then I realized, looking up, that the filter vents are completely clogged with orange grease (from the previous owner of the house, clearly), and that when very hot things are on the stove, the grease softens and falls downward into the pots.

So, obviously, I immediately dry heaved and yanked the filter vents out, and now I'm eating nothing but energy bars and ice cream, but how do I clean them properly? They're some metal-weird-soft-crunchy-NASA-like material, like a foil tarp?

You need ammonia, which I want you to promise me you'll say like *ammoooooniaaaaaaaaa*, all breathy-like. I also want you to promise me that you'll never let that ammonia go anywhere near bleach or bleach-containing products.

Those NASA-looking things will slide out, and you should put them in the sink with ammonia and water. Cold water. You probably only need about one-quarter to one-half cup of ammonia to a full sink of water. You can also add some dish soap, maybe a splurt or two? Let them soak for fifteen to twenty minutes and then rinse clean with running water. Then dry. That should do it for you, because ammonia is amazing stuff. Oh, but also! It's a fairly harsh chemical, so do use gloves when working with it.

The other things you should do, maybe while the NASA-looking things are soaking, is to go over the exterior and undercarriage of the hood with a rag that you've dipped in some ammonia and water solution and wrung out. You can dip it right in that solution you made in the sink; you have my permission to take that shortcut!

If, after cleaning the hood, you notice that the walls or cabinets surrounding the stove area are also greasy, go on and give them a wiping down with the same ammonia solution. Ammonia. It's so totally the best. Unless it's mixed with bleach, in which case it is decidedly not the best.

Oh My God There's Melted Plastic Everywhere HELP

A fairly common problem that I hear about is the havoc that is wrought when people use their oven as storage space for plastic containers, forget that they're using it as a storage space for plastic containers, turn the thing on, and go merrily about their day until the acrid smell of burning plastic smoke clues them into the fact that something has gone very, very wrong.

A quick detour to address the use of an oven for storage: this is a thing you should avoid if at all possible. While it's tempting to use that space to keep cookie sheets or baking pans or shoes, it's a terrible practice because it's so easy to entirely forget that those things are in there when you go to turn on the oven. Even things that are made of metal or glass and are ovenproof don't benefit from being in there, empty, just heatin' up. It can warp or stain them. Also, when you finally do remember that they're in there, they'll be SUPER HOT and then you'll need to put them somewhere to cool off and then also remember that they're SUPER HOT and not touch them, so just generally please use your oven for cooking and not storage. And definitely never, ever, ever use the oven to store anything plastic. I know you're smarter than that.

If, however, you had a momentary lapse of reason and find yourself with melted plastic on your hands (and in your oven), there are two routes you can take: hot or cold.

Let's start with the cold method: you'll need a giant bag of ice and will basically plant it on the area where the plastic has melted. Once the plastic has had a chance to freeze, which will shrink it, which in turn will loosen it from the oven interior, you can get it up with a sharp-edged scraper.

If you've got a gas stove, it's worth noting that you can unscrew the bottom panel of the stove, which will make cleaning it way easier. It's also essential if you're going to take the cold route, because if you put a giant plastic bag of ice on the floor of a gas stove, the heat from the pilot will melt the ice *and* the bag, which means you'll end up with more melted plastic plus a giant puddle. Like a kiddie pool in your oven! Except not at all fun. So remove the bottom panel (just be sure to turn the gas off before you do)!

The heat route is, in my opinion, the best way to go, and it's also the method you'll *have* to choose if the plastic is stuck to the side walls. Unless you want to hold the bag of ice against the side of the wall, which I don't think you want to do. It's also the way to go if you've got a gas stove that you're not up to disassembling.

To prevent the plastic from smoking, turn the oven on to the lowest heat setting possible, usually around two hundred degrees, and heat it just until the plastic is melted. Then, using a scraper tool (it needn't be sharp since the plastic is pliable), scrape up the melted plastic. If the plastic rehardens during this process, just shut the oven door and turn the heat back on until it's again melted to a point at which you can get back to your scraping.

So those are the basics of what to do about melted, stuck-on plastic in the oven, BUT LISTEN UP, even if that's *not* your problem, because these are the general instructions for dealing with melted plastic, not just when it's in your oven. For a non-oven heat source, use a hair dryer. The more you know!

So that was a fun romp through some of the issues attendant to oven-ovens, but what about the other kinds of ovens? Like the toaster kinds and the microwave kinds and the Easy-Bake kinds? Yeah, okay, mostly kidding about the Easy-Bake kind, but it's fun to remember, isn't it?

Microwave Ovens

There are loads of ways to clean a microwave oven, but before we get into it, I want to encourage you to deal with splatters and spills as they happen by wiping them with a damp sponge. I know that's an insane thing to ask for, but your life will be better off if you can do this for me. It will make me so happy!

If you don't, which I know you won't, you're going to need to clean out your microwave every now and again using more than just a sponge, because your splatters and spills have been cooked onto the surface as a result of your refusal to make me happy.

The best way to clean a microwave oven is to harness the power of steam by microwaving a bowl of something wet for two to five minutes, depending on the power of your machine—you want to get it close to or full-on boiling. Does it go without saying that you need to use a microwave-safe bowl for this? Should I say it anyway? Yeah, probably not a bad idea to say it anyway.

Once you've micro'd your something wet, remove it (CARE-FUL! It's hot.) and wipe the interior of the oven out with paper towels, a cloth, or a damp sponge. The steam will have loosened up any stuck-on food, and it will all wipe out fairly easily.

In terms of the wet things to use, you have some choices, and isn't that nice?!

- White vinegar: Mix a half cup of vinegar with a half cup of water.
- Lemon: Cut a lemon in half and place the halves cut side down in a bowl or on a plate.
- Dish soap: Mix a blurt or two into a cup of water.
- Water: If you've got nothing else on hand, plain old water with nothing else in it will work too. About a cup of it ought to do.
- All-purpose cleaners: You *can* use all-purpose cleaners for this task, but it's best to go with something more natural so you don't end up microwaving any residual chemicals into your foodstuffs.

You can wipe the turntable down while it's in the machine or remove it and hand or machine wash it.

Toaster Ovens

Toaster ovens are marvelous contraptions, but they also have hoarder-ish tendencies when it comes to things like crumbs and melted cheese drips. So it's important to clean them out every so often (how about every six months, depending on usage levels? Does that sound fair?) to prevent fires and also so as not to create a welcoming environment for critters.

First things first: unplug the toaster oven. This is, arguably, the most important step. Please do not forget to do this!

Then you'll want to take out the tray and rack(s), pitch them in your (empty) kitchen sink, and wipe any crumbs out from the bottom of the appliance. If there are a ton of crumbs, you may just want to tip the thing over your garbage can and bang on its back to dislodge them.

If the oven has a nonstick coating, which you'll know you've got from having reviewed your owner's manual *meaningful look*, wipe it down with a sponge or rag and warm soapy water. Nonstick surfaces don't love cleansers that are too harsh, nor do they care for abrasive scrubbing pads or brushes, so stay away from those.

If the interior of the oven is metal, rather than nonstick, you can use a Brillo pad or any similar branded steel wool and soap product. When you're done scrubbing at it, wipe it down with a clean, wet rag or sponge. You can also use your Brillo pad to clean the inside and outside of the oven's glass window; if there's a lot of buildup, you may also want to use glass cleaner or white vinegar to shine things up. Do not, however, use the steel wool to clean the exterior of the oven, as it can scratch, and that will look ugly, and no. Don't do that. Instead, wipe down its exterior with a damp sponge or rag; if there's greasy buildup, try a little white vinegar or a grease-cutting dish soap like Dawn. Then dry everything off with a clean rag or dishcloth.

Leave the door open to continue to let the unit air-dry while you turn your attention to the tray and rack you stashed in your sink. Go ahead and clean those as you would any dish, using hot water and soap. If there's buildup or badly stuck-on food, you can use a Brillo pad (provided the tray isn't nonstick) or a combination of baking soda and white vinegar to create a gunk-unsticking volcano effect.

Give everything one last going-over with your dry rag, put the tray and rack back in, plug the thing back in, and you're done! Oh, except for the part where you make me some cheese toast in exchange for telling you how to clean your toaster oven.

This leads us nicely into our final sprint through the horrors of keeping your kitchen clean, because God, I'm tired, aren't you? Yes? Do you want to maybe open a bottle of wine and talk about *The Real Housewives of New Jersey*? God, yes, let's do that instead of talking about how to clean those pesky small appliances in your kitchen space.

Oh. Um, sorry, no, the people who are in charge of me are saying I can't do that. (They're no fun at all.) So I guess it's back to small appliances!

Appliance	Cleaning Products to Use	What You Need to Know
Coffeemaker	White vinegar	Put a filter in the basket and run the coffeemaker with a mixture of one part white vinegar to two parts water (no coffee!). Dump the brewed vinegar water, allow the pot to cool, and then make another pot with just water. If you still smell vinegar, run another cycle of just water. Wipe the exterior with a damp cloth.
Tea/Electric Kettle	White vinegar and rice	Brew a pot of "tea" using equal parts water and white vinegar; add rice to the pot if there is buildup—the rice serves as a natural, gentle slougher.

Appliance	Cleaning Products to Use	What You Need to Know
Toaster	Dish soap; white vinegar; ammonia	Remove the crumb tray and empty it into the trash; wipe it clean with either a small amount of dish soap and a sponge, or white vinegar and a paper towel. Turn the toaster upside down over the garbage and gently bang on it (don't bang too hard or you'll risk dislodging its internal parts!) to knock loose any crumbs stuck in the unit. Wipe the exterior clean with a rag and a bit of vinegar or dish soap. Dish soap is recommended if the unit is sticky or greasy. You can also use ammonia if things are really bad.
Electric Grinder	Rice	Fill the grinder halfway up with rice, grind it, throw the pulverized rice away. Unplug the grinder and wipe any residue out with a dry paper towel.
Blender/Food Processor	Dish soap and lemon; baking soda and vinegar; ammonia	Fill the bowl of the blender or processor halfway with warm water; add half a lemon and a small amount of dish soap; blend until foamy. Rinse with hot water and dry. For cleaning serious amounts of built-up grime, use baking soda mixed with water and vinegar; follow the same instructions. The exterior of the appliance can be wiped down with soapy water, white vinegar, or ammonia.
Juicer	Dish soap, toothbrush	Make a bubble bath in your kitchen sink with hot water and a small amount of dish soap. Put all removable/cleanable parts into the bath. While the parts are submerged, use a sponge to wash them. A toothbrush will help for corners and the screen part of the filter. Drain the sink and rinse each piece in hot water. Wipe off splatters on the exterior of the machine with a damp cloth.

While kitchens can be a huge challenge to keep clean, it's also good to keep in mind that a little bit of work can go a long way. If you can tackle messes as they come up, that will help immensely. But small things like wiping off the counters and stovetop daily will also help to cut down on the amount of strenuous cleaning you'll have to do to your kitchen. It's so worth it—kitchens can be such happy places, and they'll be even happier places if you're not terrified of touching any and all surfaces.

CHAPTER 2

Cleaning Floors, Ceilings, Walls, and Other Immovable Things

In a perfect world, we could pick up our floors and throw them in the washing machine. Actually, in a perfect world, our floors would never get dirty, mold would never grow on ceilings, and humans would never projectile vomit, hitting every available surface including the walls.

But it is not a perfect world, and so it's time to talk about caring for the things in your home that are immovable and therefore a million times more frustrating to keep clean.

Floors

We're all allowed to have one chore that we absolutely *hate* and avoid for as long as humanly possible. For me that chore had long been Dealing with the Floor.

I hated all of it: vacuuming, mopping, Swiffering (oh God, don't even get me started on the homicidal rage into which the sight of a Swiffer can send me). Sweeping is *okay*. But only okay. Let's not get carried away here or anything, because there's still the maddening task of sweep, sweep, sweeping the detritus into the dustpan and auuuuuuggggggghhhhhhh. Oh God, and then with the baseboards! Why must there always be the baseboards???

The point of all of this is to acknowledge, before we even get into it, that keeping the floors clean is a beastly task. I know you're not going to like to hear this, but the truth is that the more often you do it, the less beastly cleaning the floors becomes. And you might not like to hear this, either: I used the past tense to describe my feelings about doing the floors on purpose because once I mastered the art of it? It turns out that I actually kinda like washing the floors. Shhh, though, don't go around telling people that, or I'll spend the rest of my life on my knees, and oh boy, did that ever sound not at all the way I meant it to sound!

The biggest problem I always had with the floors was that pushing a mop felt really awkward and there was always either too much or too little water slopping all over the place and OH MY GOD WHY IS THERE HAIR EVERYWHERE THAT IS NOW WET HAIR EVERYWHERE AND GROSSSSSSSSS.

Do you feel me? I bet you feel me.

And then one day I was kvetching to a similarly Clean Friend about how much I hate doing the floors, and he was all, "I do mine once a week on my hands and knees." And then I stabbed him because seriously.

But also? I'm willing to try just about anything when it comes to cleaning, and I figured the only thing I had to lose by trying out his technique was the use of my knees for an hour or so afterward.

And you already know the happy ending here, which is

that I tried the hands-and-knees approach—or as I call it because everything sounds better with a cutesy name, handsies and kneesies—and yup, it was so much better than any other way I'd tried before. It went way faster than I would have expected, made me feel like the floors were *actually* getting clean, and generally was a surprisingly painless process (except for those kneesies, ouch! I'll explain some tips on minimizing the physical pain part of things when we get into the nitty-gritty of technique).

But before you ask me, "But, like, how?"—and we'll get there, I promise!—we'll review various floor-cleaning techniques, including sweeping, three kinds of mopping (dry, wet, and steam, oh my!), and, of course, my beloved handsies-and-kneesies method—how about an overview of flooring types? And a wee primer on the cleaning products and techniques that are best suited for each? Yes, sure, let's do that! Especially since I'm forever getting questions from people being all, "So I have these floors that are, like, made of something?" and it actually really matters what your floors are made of, in terms of keeping them clean.

Wood and Laminate Flooring

What is it?

It's wood. Have . . . have you really gotten this far without knowing how to identify wood? Sorry, I'm just teasing, and actually it's good to be able to determine the difference between surface-, penetrating-, or oil-sealed and laminate flooring because they need to be treated quite differently.

To determine if you've got surface-sealed versus penetrating- or oil-sealed floors, run your finger across the floor; if there's a smudge, you've got a penetrating- or oil-sealed floor. If not, you can breathe a sigh of relief, because you've got surface-sealed floors, which are way easier to keep clean.

Surface-sealed, by the by, generally refers to polyurethane-, urethane-, or polycyclic-coated flooring. The penetrating- and oil-sealed category includes shellac, varnish, or lacquer; though they're technically surface sealants, they need to be treated the same way penetrating and oil sealants do. Also, it's okay if you don't really understand any of that. I don't really either.

Laminate flooring mimics the look of wood but needs to be treated differently from wood. A common brand name for laminate flooring is Pergo.

What should I use to clean surface-sealed floors?

- Dish soap and water solution
- Ammonia and water solution
- White vinegar or glass cleaner and water solution
- Floor-cleaning products like Pine-Sol, Fabuloso, Spic and Span, etc.

What should I *not* use to clean them?

- Excessive amounts of water
- Very hot water
- Wood furniture spray (like Pledge or Endust)
- Wax
- Abrasive cleansers

Which method shall I choose?

Sweep or dry mop first, then either damp mop or handsies-and-kneesies wash, then polish with a dry cloth. It's important to dry the floor! You really don't want water hanging out with your wood floor; it's a real bad influence and before you know it your floors will be out behind the Dumpster, cutting class and smoking cigarettes.

What should I use to clean penetrating-sealed floors?

- Broom
- Dry or microfiber mop
- Vacuum
- Wax stripper or mineral spirits to remove old wax buildup
- Liquid or paste wax

What should I *not* use to clean them?

- Water
- Acrylic- or water-based wax
- Furniture wax

Which method shall I choose?

You never want to damp mop a penetrating-sealed floor. For regular cleaning, either vacuum or sweep, and then go over the floor with a dry mop if necessary.

To keep things looking shiny and nice, every six to twelve months, go ahead and strip the old wax finish, which will dull over time, using a stripper or mineral spirits (which can be found at any hardware or home-improvement store), and refinish with either liquid or paste wax. Once the wax has been applied, buff the floors with a soft cloth, being sure to work with the grain of the wood. You can also spot treat sections of the floors with wax as needed.

What should I use to clean laminate floors?

- Dry or damp mop
- Vacuum
- Ammonia and water solution
- White vinegar and water solution

What should I *not* use to clean them?

- Excessive water
- Soap
- Wax
- Abrasives

Which method shall I choose?

Sweep, vacuum, or dry mop regularly. Laminate doesn't love water, but a deeper cleaning will be necessary from time to time, which can be done with a damp mop or cloth. Just be sure to dry each section as you go, as water left on the surface can cause warping.

Tile and Grout

What is it?

It's the square stuff in your bathroom. Okay, sorry, sorry! The actual thing you need to know about tile is that the three most common types of tile are ceramic, porcelain, and stone. Ceramic tiles are generally used in high-traffic areas like entries and hallways, whereas porcelain is generally found in bathrooms and laundry rooms, as it tends to be more water-resistant. Stone tiles are made of marble, granite, slate, etc., and need to be cleaned differently from porcelain or ceramic tiling.

What should I use to clean porcelain or ceramic tile?

- OxiClean and water
- Bleach and water
- Bleach-based cleaning products (Tilex, Clorox Clean-Up, and the like)
- Ammonia and water solution with a blurt (technical term) of dish soap, but never never never never never mix ammonia and bleach together—do you promise? I want to hear you promise!

What should I *not* use to clean it?

- Vacuum with a beater bar
- Abrasive cleansers

Which method shall I choose?

Sweep or dry mop first, then get down on your haunches and scrub that tile using a scrubber brush before wiping dry with a soft cloth. If the grout doesn't look as fully bright as you'd like, let everything dry before you knock yourself out scrubbing at it—as it dries, the grout will continue to lighten in color.

What should I use to clean stone tile?

- Dish soap and water
- Stone-cleaning products

What should I *not* use to clean it?

- Ammonia
- Vinegar
- Lemon

- Abrasive cleansers
- Oils and fats

Which method shall I choose?

Sweep or dry mop first, then mop or handsies-and-kneesies wash using a soft cloth.

Linoleum

What is it?

Linoleum is a flooring type generally made of solidified linseed oil, pine pitch, and fillers laid onto a canvas or burlap backing. Think of the stuff on the floors of sinfully ugly '70s kitchens—there's your linoleum. (Note: Sinfully ugly '70s kitchens are totally righteous, and don't you dare update them.)

What should I use to clean it?

- Dish soap and warm water
- White vinegar or window cleaner and warm water
- Ammonia and warm water
- Floor-cleaning products like Pine-Sol, Fabuloso, Spic and Span, etc.

What should I *not* use to clean it?

- Wax-based products
- Solvent-based products, which can soften and damage linoleum
- Abrasives
- Excess water
- Very hot water

Which method shall I choose?

Sweep or dry mop first, then either damp mop or handsies-and-kneesies wash with a soft rag or sponge, wiping dry when you're done to create a nice shine.

"But, like, how?"

So there are your basic floor types, which means it's time for us to get into what I call the "But, like, how?" portion of the festivities, otherwise known as "floor-cleaning techniques," but that's sort of boring, so we'll stick with "But, like, how?"

Sweeping

Grab a broom. Sweep the floor. Move all the grunge into a little pile. Sweep the little pile into a dustpan or vacuum it up. Sweeping, I feel, is highly underrated. The combo of a broom and a handheld vacuum? It's life-changing, seriously. Also? You can sweep an area rug. I bet you never thought of that, but you absolutely can. As a reminder of the way history works: people were cleaning floors, including rugs, long before vacuums—or heck, *electricity* for that matter—were invented. And what do you think they used? Ding, ding, ding! They used brooms. And also the handles of brooms to beat the ever-loving tar out of the backs of rugs to thwack out filth.

Dry Mopping

Dry mops, while they're good at what they do, are a little bit gross. They're those ones that kind of resemble a Muppet with the yarn-looking oval pads attached to a long handle. If you don't have your own washer and dryer, you can basically forget about them because that Muppet-looking pad needs to be washed frequently, and you definitely don't want to throw it in with anything other than other cleaning rags because yuck. This is because the moppy part picks up a boatload of hair and dust bunnies, and you've got a dust animal living in your home. So unless you've got your own laundry setup or a good vacuum that can get the mop head clean of all that mess, I would suggest you stick with sweeping.

If, however, you decide that dry mopping is for you, here are a few tips you should be aware of:

- Work in straight lines for the best results. So start in a corner and push the mop forward in a straight line. Then turn, overlap a small portion of the line you just cleaned with your mop, and do the same on the next section.
- Periodically clear the mop of hair, lint, dust bunnies, etc., with your hands as you mop.
- For better results, use a dry-mop spray, which will help to pick up more dirt. However, and this is really important, so after I tell you once I'm going to tell you a second time to make sure you get this, you mustn't ever use a furniture polishing spray like Pledge or Endust on your floors. Doing so will cause them to become too slick and can result in someone slipping and seriously hurting themselves. I REPEAT: you mustn't ever use a furniture polishing spray on your floors. Thank you for your attention to this important matter.

Damp Mopping

The biggest thing I want you to know about mopping is that this is a DAMP process. Not a wet one. I'm pretty sure the reason I so often hear the plaintive wail of "Jolieeeeeeeeeeee! How do I moooooooop?" is because you all are trying to mop with a sopping wet piece of equipment and no, no, no. DAMP. This is a damp process.

With that said, here's how you mop:

Regardless of which type of wet mop you choose, sponge or string, the technique is the same: put your mopping solution in a receptacle big enough to fit the mop, so . . . a bucket, the sink, your tub, a trash barrel, a punch bowl, whatever you like, really. I'm not here to dictate these sorts of things to you. (With that said, the idea of filling up your sink with filthy mopping water gives me a bad case of the squirms, so if you do that, be a pal and lie about it right to my face. "Oh, of *course* I use a bucket for my mopping solution, *of course*!")

Once you've got your receptacle up and running, it's time to stick the mop in. And for those of us with a dirty mind or, as I like to think of it, those of us who know how to live, it's also time to make some untoward comments about your mop along the lines of "Awww yeah, stick it in, baby. Plunge it!"

Who said cleaning can't be fun?

Once you're done dirty-talking your mop, it's time for the most important part of this operation: *wringing out the mop.* You have to wring it out because this is a damp process. (DAMP, NOT WET! I know you're tired of me yelling that at you, but you also keep getting it wrong, so.) Please do not soak your floors.

Once you've wrung out your mop, it's time to hit the floors. Work along the grain of the floor; push the mop forward while bearing down firmly but not overly hard. When the mop starts to feel too dry, is no longer gliding smoothly along the floor, or you notice that you're just pushing dirty water all over your floor, put the mop back in your cleaning solution, wring it a few times while submerged in the solution to release the dirt it just picked up, then remove it from the solution and wring, wring, wring, wring, wring. Then back to your mopping. Depending on how vast and/or filthy your floors are, you may need to change out your cleaning solution partway through the process. When you've mopped the entire surface, you'll want to go over it with a dry cloth to get up any excess cleaning solution and dirt and to avoid streaking.

So that's how you mop! Try it out, see if it works for you, if you like how it feels, all those important things. For whatever this is worth, I don't care for mopping. Mostly because it feels pretty awkward, but with practice it feels less awkward, which is something to consider. But I feel like mops can get super gross, as can the mopping water, and so I prefer other methods. But that's the great thing about having choices!

Steam Mops

Steam mops are fantastic for larger homes, especially ones with a lot of tile or linoleum. They're not, however, so great for wood or laminate flooring, because they can over-saturate those flooring types with water, which you don't want. If you have wood floors that are surface-sealed, you'll have better luck with steam mops, but I would highly recommend keeping a dry rag on hand, working section by section, going over the parts you've just steam mopped with the dry rag to minimize any potential warping caused by too much water.

Washing and/or Scrubbing on Your Handsies and Kneesies

I know that, despite the cutesy-sounding name I've given this technique, you still hate me for telling you that this is the best way to clean a floor. So truth time: the first time you wash a floor on your hands and knees, you'll want to kill yourself. You may even curse my name! That's okay, my feelings will be hurt, but I'll understand. But stick with it for at least a second time, when you'll be surprised to find that while, yes, you maybe want to cut yourself a little bit, it won't seem remotely as bad to you as it did the first time.

Here are the basics you need to know: you'll need a bucket filled with cleaning solution, a sponge or rag to dip in the solution, and a dry rag to polish the area you're washing. Dip your sponge or rag in the solution, wring it out, and then go over the floor in sections, sort of working a wax-on, wax-off maneuver with the wet and dry rags. Just like with mopping, you'll need to change out the washing solution when it gets really murky.

Handsies and kneesies is also the technique of choice for tile and grout, provided that they're relatively small spaces. If you have wide expanses of tile, you should think seriously about investing in a steam mop.

I know that the prospect of being knee-down on tile is pretty gruesome sounding, and to that point I've got a secret to share with you! The real trick to dealing with tile and grout is to let the cleaning products do most of the work for you. The two best options for cleaning tile and, more important, that pesky grout are bleach (or a bleach-based product) or OxiClean.

If you're using OxiClean, you'll want to dissolve a cup of Oxi in two gallons of water and pour the solution all over the floor; if you're using a bleach-based product, spray the floor liberally with it, making sure to wear rubber gloves to protect your delicate paws. Unlike wood floors, tile is an area where you should feel free to soak the surface with impunity. (Of course here I mean "impunity within reason"—don't go flooding your bathroom, please!)

Once the cleaning solution is down, *walk away*. Let it sit for fifteen to thirty minutes, then go back in with a scrub brush—this is where the scrubbing part of the handsies-and-kneesies technique comes in—and do your lil' *ch-ch-chhhh* thing with your brush. You may also want to have a toothbrush on hand to get into corners and up against the seam of the wall. Work in sections, going over the areas that you've scrubbed with a sponge or wet rag to wipe up the suds, then again over the area with a dry rag. *Then walk away again.* It might not immediately look as clean as you want it to be, but as the grout dries, you'll start to notice a huge difference.

Hoo boy, that was a *ton* of information I just threw at you, wasn't it? Would you like a chart? Yes, let's have a chart.

Flooring Type	Products to Use	Products to Avoid	"But, Like, How?"
Surface-Sealed Wood	• Dish soap • Ammonia • White vinegar • Glass cleaner • Floor-cleaning products like Pine-Sol, Fabuloso, Spic and Span, etc.	• Excessive amounts of water • Very hot water • Wood furniture spray • Wax • Abrasive cleansers	• Sweep • Dry mop • Damp mop • Handsies and kneesies
Penetrating-Sealed Wood	• Broom • Dry or microfiber mop • Vacuum • Wax stripper or mineral spirits to remove old wax buildup • Liquid or paste wax	• Water • Acrylic- or water-based wax • Furniture wax	• Vacuum • Sweep • Dry mop

Flooring Type	Products to Use	Products to Avoid	"But, Like, How?"
Laminate	• Ammonia • White vinegar *N.B. Cleaning solutions should be used infrequently on laminate floors*	• Excessive water • Soap • Wax • Abrasives	• Broom • Dry mop • Damp mop • Vacuum
Porcelain or Ceramic Tile	• OxiClean • Bleach • Bleach-based cleaning products • Ammonia • Dish soap	• Vacuum with a beater bar • Abrasive cleansers	• Sweep • Dry mop first • Handsies and kneesies
Stone Tile	• Dish soap • Stone-cleaning products	• Ammonia • Vinegar • Lemon • Abrasive cleansers • Oils and fats	• Sweep • Dry mop • Wet mop • Handsies and kneesies
Linoleum	• Dish soap • White vinegar • Glass cleaner • Ammonia • Floor-cleaning products like Pine-Sol, Fabuloso, Spic and Span, etc.	• Wax-based products • Solvent-based products • Abrasives • Excess water • Very hot water	• Sweep • Dry mop • Damp mop • Handsies and kneesies

Walls, Ceilings, and Interior Doors

I see the looks. You're thinking that you've never cleaned a wall or a ceiling and can't imagine the circumstances under which you might do such a thing and also you're very, very worried about what kind of weirdo Clean Person mumbo jumbo I'm going to come up with by way of convincing you that you need to clean your walls and ceilings.

You'd be right about the mumbo jumbo: ponder, if you will, the bathroom. Think of all the spraying and brushing and trimming and powdering and projectile vomiting (barfers, every last one of you) that takes place in your bathroom. Now stop and consider how much fallout from those activities ends up on your bathroom walls.

Convinced? No, not really. Well how about this: remember the time you knocked over a glass of red wine and it splattered all over the walls? Hurrah! Now I've got you! That would certainly be a circumstance under which you might need to know how to clean a wall, wouldn't it?!

We're going to get into a whole bunch of specifics, but first a few overall tips to consider.

Walls and ceilings—unless you're simply spot treating them—are fairly large surfaces; given that, rags (old towels, T-shirts, flannels, sheets, etc. that you've cut or ripped up into workable sizes) work better than sponges because you can cover more surface area with them. Regardless of whether you choose to use a rag or a sponge, you'll want to wring it out so it's not sopping wet with your cleaning solution before you apply it to the wall. You're not looking to saturate the wall, just to wipe it down.

Speaking of wiping things down! If you're executing a general cleaning of your walls or ceilings, it's not a bad idea to take a pass with either a dry rag or a vacuum fitted with the brush attachment to remove any loose dirt or dust. Otherwise that loose dirt or dust will turn to mud when you hit it with your damp (DAMP, NOT WET!) rag and make more of a mess.

If you've got cobwebs hanging around (heh), you can use the hose attachment.

To reach up to ceilings, wrap the straw end of a broom with a large rag, secure it with a rubber band, and use it to dust the ceiling. While you're at it, pat yourself on the back for being such a genius MacGyver!

Speaking of that ceiling! It is a common thing in bathrooms, especially the ones suffering from a lack of ventilation, to find mold growing on the ceiling. Do not leave that untreated! You don't want to be breathing in mold spores. Use the same broom technique, but with a thicker layer of rags, dipped in a one-part-bleach-to-four-parts-water solution to kill that foul mold. BUT, BUT, BUT! Please remember to be safe—before doing this, invest in a pair of safety goggles to protect your eyes. They can be found at any hardware or home-improvement store and will only run you about two bucks. A small price to pay to protect your precious eyes, yes? Yes. Goggles, wear 'em.

And finally, a brief word on Magic Erasers. I love Magic Erasers! Magic Erasers do just what the name suggests: magically erase stains and scuffs from all manner of surfaces and are fabulous on walls (less so on ceilings because of the reaching factor), but there are some things you need to be aware of before you go about Magic Erasing things willy-nilly: you must promise that *any time you even think about using a Magic Eraser* you'll test it out on a bit of wall/floor/ceiling far off in the reaches of whatever space you're thinking about Magic Erasing to ensure that it won't ruin the finish.

Since you are such an apt pupil, who even managed to pay attention during the lecture on the composition of linoleum, it's time for the class participation portion of our lesson: true tales of messes made on immovable surfaces. Hoo boy, are these ever fun/horrifying to think about having happen in your home.

The Great Ginger Beer Explosion

My boyfriend was trying to make ginger beer in our kitchen because, you know, why not? Except he put too much yeast into the glass (GLASS) bottles that he was using to ferment. We're sitting in bed one night and we hear this sound that sounds like the cabinets falling off the walls. Both bottles exploded all over the kitchen, leaving everything that wasn't in a cabinet drenched in sticky, yeasty ginger and tiny shards of glass. We washed the things that could be washed. We mopped up the excess and then went over everything a few times with all-purpose cleaner. But it's been almost a week and everything is STILL STICKY. And we're still finding glass in our hands and feet. And worse, the ants are starting to come in.

Getting it off the tiles is challenging but doable. But it's on the drywall in these slightly shiny trails that I'm afraid to attack with cleaning products because I don't want the wall to cave in or scrub off or anything. So is there anything that will get rid of sticky almost–ginger beer once and for all that's also safe on my walls?

I need some serious help with this one, because I'm two seconds away from going at the kitchen with a sledge-hammer.

Well, that sounds utterly obnoxious! I hope you beat your boyfriend soundly for his foolishness, not to mention his crimes against ginger beer.

Whenever you're facing a greasy or sticky situation in the kitchen, the thing you want to grab for is ammonia. A few things first: you'll need to use gloves when working with ammonia, because it's pretty chemical-y, and you should consider opening a window as well. Once the gloves are on and the windows are open, mix up your ammonia solution in a bowl or bucket—you'll use equal parts ammonia to water, with a splurt of dishwashing soap if you're feeling festive—and get after those surfaces. Rags work best in this situation; just wring out the rag so it's not sopping and you won't have problems with the walls caving in. You actually won't have that problem anyway unless your walls are made of cardboard, in which case they've already collapsed from the ginger beer.

If you're opposed to ammonia, you could use a cleaning solution made up of hot water and regular dish soap. Caveat emptor: this solution won't cut through sticky residue as well as the ammonia, so you're going to have to put a lot more elbow grease into things. You might consider grabbing a Dobie pad, which will help scour the grease off without scratching the surfaces you're trying to clean up.

The Uninvited Mushroom

What I thought was a dead bug (ew) on the top of our windowsill turned out to be a mushroom. Growing out of a sizable crack in the ledge. "Ew" turns to "WTF?" There's always been water damage to the wall by the window—we live on the top floor and it's been unusually rainy to boot—but we've never smelled anything peculiar before, or had any mysterious symptoms. This is the weirdest thing I've encountered. Since we never had any drips or leaks in this apartment, I didn't really bother to complain about the visible water damage, but now I'm flipping out.

Of course we will be talking to the landlord and super. But on a scale of one to eleven, how freaked out should we be? And is there anything we should do in case our notoriously slow landlord takes forever to solve the problem?

In the short term, you will be fine health-wise, but you do need to take steps to eliminate the problem because mushrooms can be dangerous in the same way mold can be. So you'll want to have it taken care of as soon as possible if you're going to continue to live in the apartment.

This really isn't something, as a renter, that you want to take into your own hands. You can remove the mushroom and treat the area, but honestly you're really better off asking your landlord to bring in—and pay for—professionals. The advice about bringing in professionals also stands for homeowners, unless you're a very, very handy homeowner, except that you'll have to be the one, rather than the landlord, to find and call the professional. The reason for this is that there is likely some pretty major structural damage going on for things to get to the point where mushrooms are growing out of the windowsill, e.g., water behind the wall and/or cracks in the exterior of the building. There is clearly a MAJOR leak if enough water has collected that fungi can grow, and the mushroom will keep coming back and worse if it's not fixed.

The Leaching, Beading Surfactant

I have a gross cleaning question! You see, a previous renter apparently used to smoke in the bathroom, and over time the smoke stains plus bathroom condensation have formed all these yellow beads on the (painted drywall) walls. They're tacky, like dried craft glue, and when I first noticed them I blamed my boyfriend for somehow peeing on the wall. Not attractive. And they're EVERYWHERE, on the walls and the ceiling.

I've tried using Windex, vinegar, and bathroom cleaner, but nothing works except scraping each bead off with my fingernail (and even then it leaves a little yellow ring). Do you have any ideas short of power-washing this room, or should I just continue to avoid touching the walls?

I'm going to dismiss the class so that I can put my head down on my very clean desk and shake with laughter for thirty or so minutes at the mental image of you berating your boyfriend for peeing on the walls.

Now that I've had a chance to collect myself, let's get back to the business at hand. It actually sounds like the problem with your walls isn't due to heavy smoking in the bathroom but rather surfactant leaching out of the latex paint used on the walls. This problem is particularly common in kitchens and bathrooms because of the high humidity in those areas of the house. To help prevent it, turn on the exhaust fan if you have one and/or open the windows as often as possible.

The Paint Quality Institute (seriously) has this to say about treating leaching surfactant:

> Wash the affected area with soap and water, and rinse. Problem may occur once or twice again before leachable material is completely removed. When paint is applied in a bathroom, it is helpful to have it dry thoroughly before using the shower. Remove all staining before repainting.

The thing is that your problem sounds like it needs something a bit stronger than soap and water. So if you're up for it, get your hands on some TSP, or trisodium phosphate, which is a cleaning agent often used to strip or prime an existing coat of paint. But, but, but! It's a serious chemical, so you'll need to use gloves, open all windows, and generally be careful with it. TSP also comes in a phosphate-free version (look for something at your local hardware or home-improvement store called TSP-PF—that's the stuff) that's slightly less toxic.

With all that out of the way, if you're *really sure* nicotine stains are what you've got on your hands (or, um, your walls, I guess) here are some ideas for getting those gone. Either bleach or ammonia—but not together! Never together!—is the thing here. However, some people are opposed to serious chemicals, which is weird but okay, I guess, and those people can mix up a vinegar solution instead. Use a large sponge, rag, or scrub brush to wash the walls, and a clean rag to dry each section as you go along.

The Devil in the (Popcorn) Walls

After a very fun, very drunk birthday, I paid for it the next morning. Long story short (I'm sure you can fill in the blanks): how do I get vomit marks off a textured wall? My wall is white and it's kind of like a toned-down popcorn ceiling wall. I blotted up all the excess moisture, but now I'm stuck with the color left behind. Help, Jolie! I don't want to look at this every day.

Oh, those lovely textured walls and ceilings that are certainly not the work of the devil during his brief stint as an interior designer. (They are.)

When you're dealing with textured walls, the primary difference in terms of care is the tool you use to clean it off; things like sponges or paper towels are going to shred instantly upon contact with a nubbly surface. So you'll want to use a rag, the sturdier the better—something like an old terry-cloth towel, cut into small pieces so it's easy to work with, would be perfect here. Also worth noting is that a good pair of rubber gloves will help to protect your hands and forearms from getting scratched up.

You can treat the stain with regular old dish soap or, if it's really stubborn, a bit of bleach. Magic Erasers are also an option except that you might experience shredding depending on how popcorn-y the wall is.

One final thing to be aware of with popcorn coating: older versions may have contained asbestos. If there's any chance *at all* that this is the case with your walls, DO NOT TOUCH THEM. Attempting to clean asbestos will release that insanely toxic stuff into your living environment even more than it already is, and you definitely don't want that. So if it's indeed a question, make sure you bring in professionals to do the appropriate testing. And then sue the living daylights out of your landlord.

The Confetti Cannon Conundrum

At my boyfriend's birthday party earlier this year, one of his friends shot off several dollar-store confetti cannons all over the place. Drink spills ensued, and the confetti dyed the hardwood floors (as well as linoleum) in numerous conspicuous places. I've tried scrubbing with dish soap and water, as well as a variety of useless stain-remover products designed for use on hardwood floors. Is there a way to remove these stains or is refinishing the floors the only option?

I propose that we all have parties that end in confetti-stained floors. What fun! Also there are a whole bunch of ways to clean up dye stains off floors, which means that we can have parties that end in confetti-stained floors with impunity. *Sets off confetti cannon*

Before we get to the options you've got for cleaning up dye stains, the usual rule applies here: test a discreet spot to ensure that the method you're going with doesn't damage the floors. With that out of the way, here are some options for you.

Ammonia and Dish Soap

Mix about a quarter cup of ammonia with one to two tablespoons of dish soap and a few cups of water, swirl that all around to make it sudsy, and use the solution to wash the floors with a sponge or old rag. A scrub brush will help move things along if the staining is present in a large area of the floor.

Rubbing Alcohol

Pour the alcohol onto a clean rag and hit the stains in a circular motion.

OxiClean

I love a stain remover with grit, which is what the powder formula is when it's mixed with water. Oxi will go a long way in lifting dye stains without harming your floors.

Magic Eraser

Magic Erasers are amazing but should be the last stop before refinishing, as they're quite likely to pull up the finish and ruin the floors. I know we already talked about this and that you promised to obey me, but as a reminder: you must, must, must test out a Magic Eraser on a bit of floor far off in the reaches of the apartment to ensure that it won't lift the finish right up. If it doesn't take the finish off, go wild and erase those stains.

Other Immovable Things

Forced Heat Radiators

Huddle around, campers. I'm going to tell you a scary story about a filthy forced heat radiator that bedeviled me. For three years—three years!—I lived with this dusty, cobwebby, filthy thing in the corner of my bedroom. Every now and again I'd stare dejectedly at it, wondering why it didn't come with a self-cleaning mechanism, before slipping back into the blessed state of grime denial I'd created for myself.

And then one day, someone asked me about cleaning forced heat radiators and I had to admit that I wasn't really sure how one would go about such a thing and was also hell-bent on figuring it out.

And figure it out I did! Fair warning: the process? SUCKS. And you know what else? Martha, Heloise . . . none of them gals are going to tell you that hard truth. But I will, because we're all friends here and friends don't let friends approach a dirty forced heat radiator without knowing all the facts.

Despite the suckage involved in this task, it's worth doing, and not just for cosmetic purposes, because all that dirt and dust and God only knows what can cause a person with allergies, asthma, or other respiratory issues major problems.

With that preamble out of the way, let's get down to it. I am truly sorry for what you're about to go through.

What You'll Need

- Rubber gloves
- Small bucket or bowl for cleaning solution
- Cleaning solution of choice (I used ammonia solution, but soapy water would work just as well, as would any sort of all-purpose cleaner mixed with water)

- A pile of thin rags (T-shirts, sheets, or dishcloths work well for this; bath towels much less so)
- A hair dryer
- Music

First move everything away from your work area. There's going to be water and muck slopping all over the place, so it really is important at the offset to move everything—books, furniture, curtains, pets—well away from your workspace.

Next up, put on some music. This is crucial to the process in that it will help to keep you from killing yourself. Not that this task will make you want to kill yourself! (This task will make you want to kill yourself.) Some other things to consider:

- Make yourself as comfortable as possible—if you've got hardwood floors, fold up a towel to sit or kneel on to give your tush and/or knees some relief.
- If you've got a bad back, take a couple of painkillers prior to starting to stave off aches and pains that will come with the weird stretching and bending this task calls for.
- If you've got allergies, make sure you've taken your allergy medication, because there's going to be a ton of dust flying and you'll be an allergic, miserable mess if you don't.
- Wear appropriate clothing. This is basically yoga with dirt, so dress accordingly.

Once you've got things set up, plop down in front of the radiator. Oh! Make sure it's turned off and cool to the touch. Starting at the top and working down, you'll want to wipe down the exterior of the unit with your cleaning solution, being careful to wring out your rags before doing so. Don't soak the radiator, because it's metal and you'll wind up with rust problems.

Once you've gone over the exterior a few times, you'll want to get in between the coils. Basically you're going to floss the radiator. So sort of roll your rag up and then stick it through the opening of the coils, then move it up and down, pulling it tight to get maximum friction. This will take some time and definitely more than one going-over for each coil. The majority of the built-up dirt is going to be at the bottom of the coils, since that's where dust settles, so pay particular attention to those areas.

I also found that dipping my begloved hands right in the cleaning solution and using my fingers to pull off dirt and grime was effective on spots that the "floss" didn't reach. But be aware that I have small fingers and that this won't work for everyone. Also, if you have small children lying about the house perhaps you could press them into service. Promise them an extra bowl of gruel as a reward.

The back portion of the coils is tricky. Depending on how the unit is configured in relation to the room, the flossing method may not be possible (it wasn't for me). Start off by turning on a hair dryer—set on cold air—facing the unit; the blowing air will help to dislodge some of the dirt coating. It won't get things off completely, but it will make it easier. If your wingspan and arm size allow for this, reach around the back end of the unit and get your fingers in there. Sort of grab at the barnacle-like dust bunnies that are clinging to the coils and then dip your digits in the cleaning solution and try to rub off as much grime as you can by wiggling your fingers.

That's really it! You may want to augment your equipment with a long, skinny-bristled brush, which will probably be rendered a one-time-use-only object when you're done with this task, but if you don't have miniature hands it will help immensely.

Good luck out there. This is the worst thing ever.

Air-Conditioning Units

There are two things to know about cleaning an air-conditioning unit; the first is that a thorough cleaning that gets at all the parts is a task that involves being quite handy. If you're not up to it, you can and should call in a professional. The second is that there are a few simple things that you should be doing regularly during air-conditioning season. These are very, very easy and will save you money because they will allow the unit to cool better and faster and also will help with summertime allergies, if you have those. Because your air conditioner won't be blowing dust and pollen into your home.

An important safety note before you go mucking about with your AC—please turn off the unit *and unplug it*. I say this out of an abundance of caution; it's pretty easy to knock the ON button and have the darn thing turn on while you're futzing, which is why I want you to take the extra step of unplugging the unit.

The few simple things are as follows:

Cleaning the screen: Take the screen out of the unit, put it in the kitchen sink or bathtub if the sink isn't big enough, and cover it with warm water and a bit of dish soap. While it's submerged, use a sponge to clean off the dirt and whatnot. Things get even easier if you have a hose attachment on your kitchen sink, which you can aim at the back of the screen, i.e., the not-dirty side, and force the grime off with just the water pressure. Once it's clear of dirt, dry it before you put it back in the unit so the water doesn't get into the machinery. It's best to use a dishcloth or rag for this task rather than a paper towel, which will get all torn up and stuck to the screen.

This is a thing you should do monthly during the time

when your AC is in regular use. It takes, honestly, less than five minutes.

Dusting the exterior unit: Dusting the unit will also help cut down on any summer allergy problems you might be having. If you've got a feather duster, great; run it over the vents to remove dust. If you're dusterless, you can use a dry cloth that you've sprayed lightly with an all-purpose cleaner and go over each vent. Just wiping down the front of the unit won't do much, honestly; you really do need to take the time to wipe out each slat. It won't take that long!

Visible innards: If you notice, when you're removing the screen, that the innards of the unit have built-up dirt on them, you can use a dryer sheet rubbed gently over the grimy areas to remove the dirt.

Ceiling Fans

Oh, well, this is so stupidly easy you're going to be mad that I even had to tell you about the secret to cleaning a ceiling fan: get an old or cheap pillowcase that you're willing to donate to your cleaning pile, spray the inside of it with all-purpose cleaner or a dusting product, put the open end around the blade, and slide the case down its length, grip tightly and pull it back. *Et voilà!* All the dust will come off right into the pillowcase, meaning it won't get all over the area under the fan.

Don't you just love it? It's okay if you don't; I love it enough for both of us.

Carpeting and Area Rugs

First things first for my fine carpet-having friends: if you live in a home with carpeting, please have a carpet cleaning product like Resolve or its ilk on hand, because you will inevitably make messes. If you accept that at the outset, things are going to be a lot better for you down the road. OxiClean is also great on carpeting if you want to reduce the number of products you're keeping in the home, or if you've ignored what I just told you about taking the preemptive measure of having carpet cleaner on hand. Also, I'm hollering at you, "I WON'T BE IGNORED, DAN." Later I'm going to boil your bunny. Don't worry, I'll clean the pot out when I'm done.

Another thing that I'd encourage you to accept now: with the exception of mud, which is best treated when it's dry and can be vacuumed or brushed up, pretty much anything, stain-wise, that you get on carpeting really needs to be dealt with as soon as possible.

Oh right, vacuums. If you have carpeting, you really ought to own a vacuum. If money and/or space is an issue for you, look for what's called a "stick" vacuum, which is fairly narrow and can be stored easily, and will generally cost in the $50–$100 range but can be found for as low as $25–$30, especially if you keep an eye out for sales at big-box-type stores.

But back to those carpet-cleaning solutions! The good news about carpet-cleaning products is that they do much of the work for you, especially if you're prompt about triage. You should follow the manufacturer's instructions since products vary greatly, but your general procedure will be something like this: spray the stain and then let the product do its work for the recommended amount of time (usually five to fifteen minutes) before rubbing gently, so as not to grind the stain into the carpet, with a damp cloth or sponge.

Depending on what the nature of and how bad the stain is, it might be necessary to rinse and wring the rag a few times. If the stain is really bad, or if your carpet needs an all-over freshening up, steam cleaners are great and worth the price of rental—which is, believe it or not, one of the most common questions I'm asked! Yes! Yes they are wonderful and worth it! Also, they're not as expensive as you think, generally running about $30. The more you know!

Wow, that was a lot of expounding on the care and keeping of floors and walls and other immovable things. I sort of want to collapse in a heap now. Do you want to collapse in a heap too? Well, then it's a good thing the floor is so clean!

CHAPTER 3

Le Pissoir (Because These Things Sound Fancier in French)

There's nothing pretty about cleaning a bathroom. I'm not really even going to try to convince you of the good time to be found in washing up the place where everyone goes to wash themselves up. *And to do a few other things. Ahem.*

Except that . . . there's this thing that's used to clean bathrooms and, you guys? I really, really love it. Like, I *delight in it*. It's called Scrubbing Bubbles, and it is just about the best thing going. Here's what you're gonna do: go to the store and buy a can of Scrubbing Bubbles. Bring it home. Shake it up real good and then spray it all over your tub, tile walls, sink basin and ledge, and the toilet environs. Then go have a cold drink, or a cup of tea if it's chilly out. Mostly I just want you to enjoy yourself for fifteen or so minutes while the bubbles do their scrubbing.

After you've had a nice quiet moment to yourself, you'll head back into the bathroom with a damp sponge. A rag will work too, but I find a sponge far superior when it comes to working with the Bubbles. You're going to wipe down all the surfaces you covered with the Scrubbing Bubbles, followed by a quick once-over to dry everything off and pick up any lingering lint or whatnot with a paper towel, and GASP WITH DELIGHT at how freaking easy it just was to clean the darn bathroom. Then you'll consider sending me a gift to thank me for sharing with you this marvel of cleaning. (My ring size is 5½, my shoe size is 6, my birthstone is peridot, and I'm partial to stargazer lilies.)

"But, Jolie," I can hear you cry, "I can't reach into the farthest corner of my tub! How can I reap these magical benefits?"

You know those long-handled scrubbers they sell for getting your back clean? Yeah, I just blew your mind, right? Grab one of those and dedicate it to your home cleaning efforts.

"But, but, Jolie," your cries continue, "I've got hard water, and it's making a mess of everything!"

Well, here I am to explain hard water and its effects to you, starting with this: hard water contains a high mineral count, as opposed to soft water, which contains a low mineral count. Hard water isn't harmful to us human folk, though it is harmful to machinery and pipes and such because those minerals build up and leave behind what's called *scale* or *fouling* (we often refer to it colloquially as *scum*). The other important thing to know about hard water is that it doesn't play as nicely with soap as does soft water. The result of this is that when you're washing anything—dishes, hands, hair, whatever—in hard water, you'll notice a distinct lack of lather. Unless! You enlist the aid of a water softener designed to reduce the effect of minerals commonly found in hard water.

If you've got hard water, some brands of water softener to look out for are Calgon Water Softener and Charlie's Soap Laundry Booster and Hard Water Treatment. Borax will also work to combat the ill effects of hard water. If you're outside the States and can't find the brands I've mentioned, what you want to look for is a product called washing soda, the primary ingredient of which is sodium carbonate. You may need to look for it by ingredient rather than name, since the term *washing soda* may not be universal. Often they will come in tablet form, so be ready for that.

If you can't find washing soda, go on and try baking soda—which, as you'll hopefully remember from science class is sodium *bi*carbonate—it should certainly be easy enough to find pretty much anywhere overseas. It won't work *quite* as well as sodium carbonate, but because it's so universal it's well worth mentioning as an option to go with in a pinch. IMPORTANT BEAUTY BONUS NOTE: If you've found yourself in a hard-water situation after having been in a soft-water sort of place, you may notice that your hair is not behaving in the way you've grown accustomed to. Go on and mix some baking soda into your regular shampoo, which will help combat the effects of hard water on your hair.

And, finally, white vinegar is the trick to keep your machines and pipes free of buildup. (It's also the thing you're going to use if you've got soap scum buildup. If the soap scum is really bad, combine the vinegar with baking soda and/or dish soap for even more fighting power.) You can run it through your dish- or laundry washers, or use it along with a toothbrush to scrub the taps and screens on your sink faucet and on the showerhead to remove the scum. Okay, are we cool with hard water? Yup? Coooool.

"But, but, but, Jolie!" *God*, you people, with the incessant crying! "I don't even know how to clean a toilet, much less deal with smells and mold, and what in the world am I to do when the drains stop working??"

Not to worry, kiddo, I'm here for you.

How to Clean a Toilet

There are two main things you need to know about cleaning a toilet: (1) it is both a fast and easy, easy task; (2) the more often you do it, the less gross the job is. You're going to think me a terrible nit for saying so, but cleaning your toilet two to four times a month is the standard you should aim for. If you're a man reading this book, you just laughed at my pun. I hope.

You need a few things on hand before you start, but really only a few. Would you like a list? Sure you would!

- Cleaning product
- Sponge or rag
- Toilet brush
- Paper towels
- Rubber gloves

The gloves are optional but recommended because, well, you're cleaning a dirty toilet. Methinks I needn't go further than that.

Apply your cleaning solution of choice (I'm partial to Scrubbing Bubbles, and by partial I mean I love it so much I want to marry it) to the entire commode—seat, lid, top of the tank, handle, bowl—walk away for five to ten minutes, then come back and wipe everything down with a damp sponge or rag, whichever you prefer. More often than not, when it comes to cleaning, you'll want to work from the top down; the toilet is no exception. Start with the lid, move to the exterior of the tank, then the top of the seat lid, the inside of the seat lid, the top of the seat, flip the seat up and get under the bottom of it, then the rim of the bowl, then if you're feeling really, really ambitious about things, wipe the base of the toilet. Save the inside of the bowl for last.

Hit the bowl with a bowl brush, which you can wet in the toilet water even though that sounds gross. (The toilet water is actually pretty clean.) Give the entire bowl a good *ch-ch-chhh* scrubbing, paying particular attention to the hard-to-reach lip under the rim of the bowl. That's where mold and other foul things like to reside.

The last step is to grab a paper towel or two and go over the whole exterior of the toilet with it to remove any lint that the sponge or rag might not have gotten; once that's done, flush to give the bowl a rinse.

If you have a toilet with rust stains or hard-water buildup or anything that doesn't seem to want to come off in the course of your regular scrubbing routine, you should get yourself a pumice stick designed specifically for household cleaning. They're hard enough that they'll remove rust or mineral deposits, but not so hard that they'll scratch the porcelain. And isn't that a handy thing to know?! They also work on porcelain tubs and sinks that are stained, usually from hard-water deposits.

Of course I can't let you go without reminding you of the most important part of the toilet in terms of cleaning. Do you know what it is? I'll give you a moment. No? Okay: it's the handle. Think about it for a second. Right, then! We'll all agree to clean the handle!

How to Clean a Toilet Brush

It's funny to imagine the look on a person's face when it occurs to them that they've never cleaned the thing they use to clean the other things in their home, like oh, let's say . . . a toilet brush. Cleaning a toilet brush every now and again is probably a pretty good thing to do, despite most of us not really thinking on it too much. That's how most of us will be, but I can't send you out in the world without telling you that there are people who believe that after every use of a toilet brush—every single use!—that brush is to be disinfected with bleach and boiling water. I want you to be ready for those people when they spring up unbidden in your life.

With that said, if you are or would like to be the sort of person who cleans the toilet brush with bleach and boiling water after each use, by all means you should do that! I'm not here to dictate, just to help you along in your cleaning endeavors to the extent you want my help. (Though I do wish you'd wash your kitchen and hand towels more often. But! Not dictating! Just . . . maybe wincing at your personal choices a little bit.)

Those of you who are joining me in the I Will Not Bleach and Boil My Brush Every Time corner of the ring can do this as frequently or infrequently as you wish: spray the brush down with the disinfecting spray of your choice, let it sit for five or so minutes, turn the tap in the tub onto the hottest setting you can get it and rinse the brush under the hot water. You can also wash the base in which the brush sits in a similar way. But then maybe when you're done with that, think about cleaning the tub. You're doing that regularly anyway, right? RIGHT?? Right.

Smells, a Frank Discussion

Smells happen. Especially in bathrooms. And so we're going to talk about them. Now.

Sometimes a bathroom retains what is known in the business as a "sort of pissy" smell. If you're having that sort of problem, (1) I'm sorry and (2) here are a few things to consider.

The toilet itself might be the problem.

The tank part of the toilet may be the culprit. Cleaning it is
pretty easy, too, so if you suspect a problem odor is coming
from the tank, here's what to do: pour white vinegar in the
tank, a cup to a cup and a half depending on how high the
water level is—you want to make sure you leave room for
displacement when you get in there to scrub things. Well.
You're not actually going to get in there because that would
be both gross and impossible, but your hands are. Put on a
pair of rubber gloves, grab a scrub brush, and scrub out the
interior of the tank. Then flush! Once the water has stopped
running, add another half a cup of vinegar to the tank and
flush again. Repeat this as necessary—the flushing part of
things will serve to rinse the bowl with vinegar too, which
will attack any smells in other parts of the toilet that need to
be forced out. The last step is to go around the exterior of the
bowl with a rag and some vinegar solution to get up any residue lurking there.

The floor around the toilet might be the problem.

If there are men and/or children (same thing) using the
bathroom in question it's likely that the floor surrounding
the toilet, especially if it's a grouted area, is retaining the
offending pee-pee smell. So! Try washing them with a
nice cleaning solution that is appropriate to the flooring
type (see chapter 2 for more on that exciting topic!), paying
particular attention, through the use of a scrub brush or
toothbrush, to the grout. In extreme cases, the grout may
need to be redone, though I do believe that to be a pretty extreme thing, so please don't go into convulsive fits upon reading that.

The walls around the toilet might be the problem.

Let's be honest. Sometimes, the men and/or the children? Direct their pee such that it ends up on the walls. Which is horrible to think about, but if you suspect this might be the case, grab a rag and some white vinegar mixed with water and wipe those walls down to remove anything that might be causing your lingering odor issues.

Okay, so that was sort of horrifying for everyone involved, which means it's time to move on to the much less offensive topic of preventative measures. Hurrah for preventative measures! We love those!

The first rule of preventing lingering smells in the bathroom is to ensure that there's proper air circulation. This can be tricky, because if your bathroom doesn't have a built-in exhaust fan and it stinks, the last thing you want to do is leave the door open and pollute the rest of the house. But that potty needs air circulation! So: if there's a window, open it! Leave the door open, even just a crack! Put a fan in there if you can!

Once you've got some circulation in there, you can bring in some outside help. There are these things called odor-absorbing sponges that are great and can be easily tucked away in a corner, out of sight. Some easily found brands are Bad Air Sponge, Fresh Wave Odor Eliminating Crystals, and DampRid Odor Genie, but there are a whole heap of them out there. *Odor-absorbing sponge* or *crystal* are the keywords you'll want to use if you're searching for a product online or are asking for help in a store. Which, by the way, you should always do. Ask for help! But ask it of someone who works for the store, because apparently I have one of those faces that makes people think I know everything and am friendly, and I can't tell you how irritating it is to be turned into an in-store adviser when I'm just trying to pick up some paint chips and a new tin of Goo Gone.

Another type of product worth checking out is what's known as an activated carbon odor absorber, which also goes by the names *active carbon*, *active charcoal*, or *activated charcoal*. Check out a brand called Innofresh; they make all manner of wonderful activated carbon products to help you deal with your odors.

If your smell problem is specific to mold or mildew, you'll want to look into a desiccant, which is a fancy name for a substance that creates or maintains a state of dryness, to help with the root of the problem. How about some brand names? Yes, some brand names would be helpful, I think! DampRid is a common one, as is Keep It Dry; you can also buy loose silica, which is that stuff that comes in the little packets in your shoes and new handbags with the sinister warning DO NOT EAT. So please do not eat it! You can set the loose silica out in a bowl or jar or any other sort of container you've got lying around. Also, if you have pets and/or small children you'll need to be mindful about where you place desiccants, or opt for a small dehumidifier instead. Which is the perfect excuse for me to mention to you that the home-improvement stores of the world carry small dehumidifiers that are meant for use in small places like bathrooms. Now you know that! We're learning so much here, isn't it a delight?!

Since we're on the subject of learning and desiccants, a word that I obviously cannot use often enough, do you know that moisture-loving plants like ferns can also help reduce the ill effects created by excess water in areas with poor ventilation, which is nice for people with a green thumb and/or a love of flora! Also, if you are a botanist or someone with a modicum of sense you probably could have figured that out on your own, but lie to me and pretend this is revelatory.

With the subject of desiccants exhausted, it's time to turn our attention to the topic that started this all in the first place. Mold. It's real, real bad stuff, guys. But stick with me and we'll get through it okay, I promise.

Mold, Mildew, and Other Lurking Bacteria

Without turning this into too much of a science lesson, mold and mildew are essentially equivalent things, whereas bacteria is another thing altogether, though they're all closely enough related that they probably shouldn't get married and have babies. There are a bazillion (rough count) different strands of bacteria, but blessedly only one that we're going to talk about here.

But first let's take on the dreaded question of mold.

There are two solid reasons for getting after mold in the home as soon as you spot it. One, it's gross. That's a pretty good reason, right? But also it's kinda bad for you! Don't take it from me, please allow the Centers for Disease Control and Prevention (CDC) to scare the bejesus out of you:

> In 2004 the Institute of Medicine (IOM) found there was sufficient evidence to link indoor exposure to mold with upper respiratory tract symptoms, cough, and wheeze in otherwise healthy people; with asthma symptoms in people with asthma; and with hypersensitivity pneumonitis in individuals susceptible to that immune-mediated condition. The IOM also found limited or suggestive evidence linking indoor mold exposure and respiratory illness in otherwise healthy children.
>
> A common-sense approach should be used for any mold contamination existing inside buildings and homes. The

common health concerns from molds include hay fever–like allergic symptoms. Certain individuals with chronic respiratory disease (chronic obstructive pulmonary disorder, asthma) may experience difficulty breathing. Individuals with immune suppression may be at increased risk for infection from molds. ["Facts about Stachybotrys chartarum and Other Molds," Centers for Disease Control and Prevention]

You'll likely have heard the term *black mold*, which is a term used for the super, super bad sorts of mold. But actually mold comes in many colors, which is why you should put on Dolly Parton's "Coat of Many Colors" and sing to your mold as you murder it, "My mold of many colors/That my shower made for me. . . ." Or if Morrissey is more your style perhaps you could croon "Mold Is Murder" at it? You should find your own groove is what I'm trying to say here, but feel free to have some fun. Ridding the home of mold is a fairly unpleasant task, so if you can find ways to make it a little less heinous, I want to encourage you to do so!

Which brings us to the "BUT HOW??" portion of our show. There are a couple of ways to kill mold, the best of which is through the use of bleach. "But, Jolie," you're saying, "bleach is so bad for the environment!" Right, and mold is so bad for *you*. But fine, if you want to be one of those altruistic sorts, I'll give you some alternatives to bleach. The thing you need to know, you filthy hippie, is that the more eco-friendly products—tea tree oil being the best of the bunch, followed by white vinegar—used to kill mold aren't going to be as effective, will take longer to eliminate the problem, and you'll have to work harder, elbow grease–wise. Which is totally okay! Good for you for being such an exemplary steward of our planet. But it's only fair of me to let you know about the extra work involved.

If you decide to bite the bullet and use bleach, you'll want to mix it with some water in a spray bottle, or buy a product like Tilex that already comes in a spray bottle, so you can spray all the moldy areas heavily. (You know, because you've already been told, that you need to use gloves and ensure you're in a ventilated area when working with bleach, but I do like to remind you.) Allow the bleach to sit for twenty to thirty minutes; I like to think of this as marinating the mold. Once the bleach has had a chance to work its magic, go in after the spots with a heavy-duty scrubber brush. You'll probably also want to have a toothbrush on hand to help work the mold out of tight corners. If you've got tricky patches of mold, you might want to use a cream-based product that contains bleach, like Soft Scrub. Since you're wearing gloves, go ahead and use your finger to push the cream all over the patch. If you don't have the same contentious relationship with Cling Wrap that I have, you can also put a goodly amount of bleach on those patches, cover the area with the plastic wrap to hold the bleach in place, and leave it be for a few hours. It will probably all be gone without your even having to scrub at it! The same basic techniques also apply to the use of tea tree oil or vinegar, if those are the solutions you've gone with.

Now that we've talked about mold, it's time to talk about that orange, sometimes pink, stuff that's also commonly found hanging around in bathrooms. As you might suspect but have not yet confirmed, the orange, sometimes pink, stuff is no good. And you'd be right! It's bacteria. See? I told you there would be bacteria! Also it has a name: *Serratia marcescens* (don't ask me to say that out loud; *I have no idea*.)

Happily, *Serratia marcescens* is more fallible than mold, so far less elbow grease is required to clean it. Bleach will kill it, as will Lysol. Hydrogen peroxide and white vinegar will also do the trick.

In addition to killing the mold and bacteria with chemicals or salad dressing, there are some things you can employ that will help stave off its growth. We've already talked about moisture-absorbing desiccants, but if your bathroom suffers from a lack of ventilation, consider getting a small dehumidifier or a clip-on fan to reduce the amount of moisture in the room. Keeping your shower clean and dry will also make a huge difference; squeegeeing the shower walls when you're done with your ablutions will discourage the growth of mildew and mold and will also extend the life of your last major shower cleaning.

If you have a plastic shower curtain, close it fully after every shower, which will allow water to drip off, rather than collecting in the folds and giving mold a happy home in which to live. While we're on the topic of plastic shower curtains: the easiest way to clean such a thing, especially one that's gotten mildewy, is to throw it in the washing machine with laundry detergent and a half cup of bleach on a cold water setting. If you've got a top-loading machine, include a towel or two to serve as buffers to prevent the curtain from ending up in tatters from the center agitator. Once it's clean, rehang it to let it drip-dry; don't put it in the dryer, it will melt. You could also go the lazy route, as I do (this is me giving you permission to go the lazy route!), and spray down the curtain while it's still hanging, let some bleach do its bleach thing, then go back in with a damp sponge and wipe the thing down about fifteen minutes or so later.

Drains

Since you're still here, I can tell I'm going to need to up my gross-out game, which means it's time to . . . DRUMROLL, PLEASE! . . . deal with your clogged-up drains! Wheeeeeeee! Aren't we having fun?!?!

Stopped-up drains happen, and they're a bummer. If I can impress upon you just one thing from our discussion of clogged-up drains it's this: as soon as you notice that the water is draining slowly, GET RIGHT ON IT. A slow drain is a pretty painless fix, but a stopped-up one will—real talk—absolutely suck to clear.

Before you go trying to clear out your pipes, it's a good idea to find out what type of piping you have; the most common kinds of piping are plastic, iron, and copper. If you're going to use a chemical solution to fix your clog, you'll need to pick a drain clearer according to the type of piping you've got so that you don't end up with even bigger problems on your hands.

With those two important items out of the way, let's talk about preventative measures first. Baking soda and vinegar, together in perfect harmony just like ebony and ivory, is the first line of defense both in preventing clogged drains and dealing with drains that are beginning to run slowly. Plus there's that super fun volcano thing that happens, and I think we can all agree that the volcano is good, wholesome fun for the whole family.

Prevention-wise, go on and hit your pipes with a half cup of baking soda followed by a half cup of vinegar once every month/every other month depending on what your hair, etc., situation is like. Let it work through the drain for fifteen to thirty minutes and then flush with hot, hot water. It's a pain in the tush to remember, but it will make your life so much better in the long run.

If you wind up with a slow-running drain, go ahead and start the process of clearing up the stoppage with the same baking soda and vinegar formula, but repeat the process two to three times as necessary until the water is again running swiftly. You may also want to bring out your plunger, which works on sink and tub drains as well as toilets. Did you know that? I needed Bob Vila to tell me that, so don't feel bad if you considered the plunger only for use in the latrine.

If the clog is bad, i.e., water is backing up and barely draining and the plunger hasn't touched it, it's time to consider a chemical pipe cleaner.

Which brings me to this confession: it's not a popular thing to say, but I love Drano. I feel like especially if you have long hair you really have to have a drain-clearing solution on hand before backups get out of control. If I were a better person, I'd follow my own advice and clear my drain out with baking soda and vinegar once a month, but in reality every three or so months I notice my drain is starting to run slowly and reach under the sink for my beloved jug of Drano. Now you know my dirty secret.

Chemical pipe cleaners come in different forms, the most common kinds being liquid and crystal clearers. There's a brand of crystal clearer called Thrift Drain Cleaner that people SWEAR by. If you've got a wicked bad clog on your hands that even Drano or its ilk won't touch, which absolutely happens, by the way, and aren't mentally prepared to snake the drain (we're going to get to that, don't fret! Or rather: FRET), consider the crystal.

If the gentleness of baking soda and vinegar or a plunger *and* the muscle of chemical clearers fail you, it's time to bring in some brute force in the form of drain snakes.

Before we get into the whys and wherefores of drain snaking, however, another confession: I do not snake drains. I'll do a ton of gross things, but I have my own personal boundaries and I'm not ashamed of them. I'm going to circle back to this in a sec, so those of you who would like to join me in establishing Do Not Snake as a personal choice should hang tight. I'll get right back to you.

The rest of you can come over here with me.

There are three main types of drain snakes, and it's actually important to understand the differences between them. If you can't remember the difference when you're sprinting into the hardware store in a frenzy, at the very least stop someone who works there and tell them where your backup is happening and ask which snake you need. I have a friend who had a seriously backed-up toilet who went to the hardware store, came home with a snake designed for sink and tub drains, and had to turn right back around to go back for the other kind of snake. Don't let this happen to you!

(Are you panicked? I want you to be panicked, because that's how you'll remember things.) Now that you're panicking, here are the things you need to know about snakes:

Hand snakes, also called cable or hand augers, are the ones you want for clogged sink or tub drains. A twenty-five-foot snake will do you just fine, though they are available in models up to one hundred feet long.

The snake, which is actually a steel cable that's been wound around a spool fitted with a hand crank, goes down the drain and will pick up all the hair and gunk and whatever else might be clogging things up. If you're new to snaking you may want to check out one of the many, many, many videos demonstrating the technique that can be found on YouTube.

A closet auger is the one you want for snaking toilets. It's also got a hand crank, just like the cable ones, but the cable is encased in shaft and the auger part of this—at this point I should admit that even I've lost the thread here and am sort of repeating words I've learned blindly at you—is bent at all sorts of angles, allowing it to get into the weird twists and turns of a toilet's plumbing architecture. Basically the thing you need to know here is that the ones for toilets are *different*.

The last kind of snake to know about is an electric power auger, which is what you'll use if you've got a huge clog on your hands. When I say *huge clog*, I'm talking about the kinds of clogs that happen when tree roots or other enormous things get up into your pipes. The electric power auger is essentially the same thing as a cable auger, but with a motor attached to it. Unless you work in the plumbing industry—in which case, why are you here wasting your time on Drain Snaking 101?—this is a thing you'll rent, not buy.

Which brings me back to the group of Committed Snake Eschewers who have been waiting so patiently: when bad clogs happen? It's absolutely okay to call the plumber.

Now, then, that wasn't too bad, was it? I bet you thought our discussion of bathroom cleaning would be far more scarring! But other than the mold, and the hair, and the smells . . . okay, yeah, I guess maybe this was scarring for you. (Maybe now isn't the time to tell you that there's more hair to come?) But, hey, wait! You know what I can tell you that should be a great comfort? Your tub is cleaner than it's ever been, so go ahead and put on some Reiki healing music and treat yourself to a restorative bubble bath.

CHAPTER 4

Get Rid of Your Ladies, Seriously, They Are Revolting

One of the common refrains I hear from the menfolk out there is that they feel they get a super bum rap when it comes to having a reputation for being revolting. In fairness, men *are* revolting, and later on down the line we'll get into just how revolting they are; right now you should be bracing for some serious squicks, by the way—it's gonna get real, real hairy! But first, and please admire my effortless segue back to the common refrains of the menfolk with regard to the relative filthiness of the fairer sex: the hair, you guys. Every male friend of mine who's lived with women, whether it be a roommate or a girlfriend or a sister/mother/grandmother/great-aunt Ethel has come to me, fretting in hushed tones, "The hair, Jolie. Good God, *the hair.*"

And the hair isn't all, I'm sorry to report. (No, that's a lie; I'm not at all sorry to report that because if it wasn't true I'd be out of a job and I really, really like this job.) There's also the stacks of doggy-lookin' magazines everywhere, including and especially in the bathroom, where they pick up all manner of filth. And the makeup debris. And the makeup brush debris. And the fine film created when you spray your hair products all over the place (I can't be the only one still using Aqua Net, can I?).

With that soliloquy on the nature of the war between the sexes out of the way, first things first: we need to talk about the stray strands of hair dancing the minuet through your home. Then we'll get into more specific and less horrifying hair-related cleaning topics.

But back to that hair: it's . . . a big problem, those hairble-weeds that go drifting about the home if one isn't ever mind-ful of staying one step ahead of migrating clumps of hair. Now, then, you may think I'm being harsh here, but I've got a headful of Rapunzel hair that just loves to detach itself from my head and go roaming all around my apartment, so I'm speaking from a place of empathy, truly. And the best cure I can prescribe is a combination of a handheld vacuum and constant vigilance.

My strategy is to do a once-over on my bathroom floor with a handheld vacuum every day/every other day, depend-ing on how sheddy I've been and what I've got planned by way of in-home entertainment. To make things easy, store the handheld vacuum in or near the bathroom and wait to do your daily cleanup until *after* you've done your hair.

What doesn't work is wet mopping, which will only serve to adhere the hair further to the floor. And no one wants that. Dry Swiffers are an option, but honestly I don't even like to talk about Swiffers, so if you go that route, be a love and don't mention it in my presence.

Since we're on the topic of hair, let's sit with a cup of tea and talk for a spell about cleaning the things we use to make our hair look awesome, shall we? Hairbrushes, hair dryers, flat irons, hot rollers, alllllllllllllllllllll those kinds of things.

Here's a typical question that I'd bet a bunch of you have never thought of but will read and be all, "Oh sweet Sassoon, why haven't I ever cleaned my hairbrush ew ew ew I need to go clean my hairbrush RIGHT NOW." Right? Right.

Hairbrush Gunk Removal

How do you clean your hair brush? Mine always ends up with this gunky, gray gross stuff at the bottom of the bristles which I assume is a combination of dirt and dead skin held together by old sweat. GROSS. This brush is a cushion hairbrush, but I have the same problem with my round hairbrushes. How do I clean it so that when I brush my hair after I shower I don't immediately dirty it again? I regularly pull the dead hair off the brush and sometimes I pick the gunk out with my fingers, but it is just TOO GROSS. Tell me there is another way! So far my ideas are:

1. Put hairbrushes in the dishwasher. (Is this safe? Will this work?)
2. Throw them away, they are disgusting.
3. Continue to pick out the gray gunk with my fingers even though it is gross.

Am I the only one with this problem? Does everyone else know how to do this properly and I just missed that day in school?

I don't think you missed a day of school, no. I do think, as I mentioned in the lead-up to this answer, that cleaning a hairbrush just isn't one of those things we think about too much. But it's pretty important to do, because as you said, TOO GROSS. We don't want to be brushing old hair, grease, oil, products, dust, what-have-you into our clean hair, and also it will lengthen the life span of your hairbrush, on which some of us spend a pretty penny, if you do some light upkeep.

First let's back it up and talk about some daily maintenance: you should clean the hair out of your hairbrush every day. Is that a lot to ask? Maybe. But try committing yourself to this practice for one month. After that it will probably be second nature to clean your hair out of your brush after every use. You can either use a comb to rake the hair from the bristles, or your hand (I use the latter technique and it works just fine, and since it's my own hair I don't find it particularly icky).

Deeper cleaning should be done once a month, if you can manage it. It's unlikely that you'll actually do this once a month, but it's my job to tell you that that's how often you *should* perform this ritual. Once a quarter or once every six months is probably more realistic, though, right? Sure, let's go with that. To deep clean your brush you have two options, depending on what kind of brush you're using. If your brush is entirely made of plastic you can go on and throw it in the dishwasher. Just make sure to clear it well of hair so that your strands don't clog up your dishwasher because TOO TOO GROSS, am I right?

If your brush is made up of anything *other* than plastic, you'll want to hand wash it, which is a blessedly simple process, so if you're unsure just go with this method: fill a medium-size bowl or your bathroom sink with warm water and a few drops of shampoo, preferably something gentle like baby shampoo. Baby shampoo, by the way, is a product that's highly recommended for cleaning up all sorts of beauty products, and it's relatively inexpensive (plus, for cleaning, a little bit goes a long way) so go ahead and grab a medium-size bottle and tuck it under your sink with the rest of your cleaning products. Always a good thing to have on hand in a beautifying chamber. Next, swirl the brush around in the sudsy solution and, if necessary, use a soft-bristled tooth-brush to scrub the bristles free of any built-up gunk. Drain, rinse, and refill the sink with clean water, and swirl the hair-brush until clean of suds. Place it on a dry towel, bristle-side down, and allow to dry. The drying process may take up to twelve hours, so factor your plans to look gorgeous into your cleaning schedule.

As to the question of round brushes, I'm going to confess something at the risk of my Clean Person cred, in the hopes that the confession makes you feel better about not know-ing things, because no one should be expected to know ev-erything, and a big important thing I want you to get out of this book is that it's okay not to know something! Seriously, you all are way too hard on yourselves. Here goes: I could not EVER sort out how to successfully clean a round brush. So I did what any enterprising writer would do and I crowd-sourced the answer on Twitter (oh, hey! Are you on Twitter? You should follow me @joliekerr; we'll have a whole heap of fun!), and here's what I found out: many people use a pick comb to get under the matted hair, lift it up, and pull the loosened clumps out with their hands. Now, then, I'd tried the comb method and could never make it work for me, but I also wasn't specifically using a pick comb. I can see now that a pick comb would make the process much, much easier, given its thin, widely spaced tines. But another suggestion was made, and a million lightbulbs went on over my head— cut the matted hair out with a pair of scissors. Right?? And from my perspective, as a person who needlepoints and therefore has a million pairs of tiny embroidery scissors in my home, this was a perfect solution.

And it really was a perfect solution; in less than a minute I had a round brush entirely void of hair that I could then wash in the same manner as described to wash a flat brush. Boom! So exciting!

Now, then, the question asker mentioned something about hair school and that got me thinking about all the other things we use on our hair that we should know how to clean. Because between our own hair oil and the products we use and the dust that's lurking around all of our homes, these things can get pretty messed up. And then they won't work as well! And also eeew you don't really want to put that filthy thing in/on your hair, do you? No, you do not.

Flat/Curling Iron

I'm gonna give you two methods for cleaning a flat or curling iron. One is DUMB EASY. One is just plain easy, but more *official*, so I feel like I need to tell you about both processes and let you choose for yourself if you want to follow the rules or if you want to be a REBEL. (Be a rebel. Go on. You know you want to.)

Let's start with the plain old easy method, which, *God*, live a little, would you?? You'll need a microfiber cloth and water, for this. Maybe a cotton swab. We'll see how things go.

To clean, unplug your iron and dampen the microfiber cloth; wipe the exterior of the iron and the plates clean. That's it! If there's buildup that a once- or twice-over with the cloth didn't get up, use a cotton swab dipped in water to clean the crevices.

So that's the proper method. Would you like to hear the improper method? Of course you would! My hairdresser told me this one. But before I repeat it to you I do want to ask you to be careful if you're going to go this route, because I wouldn't want you burning yourself. The improper method is to wipe the *already hot* iron clean with an ever-so-slightly damp cloth or towel. Just make sure you've got enough thickness to protect your hand—think along the lines of an oven mitt, about that thick. I like this method because (1) it's easy and (2) the combination of the damp cloth and the hot styling tool produces steam, and steam is a wonderfully effective way to clean and sanitize things. You can make this part of your daily routine, too, since it will add on fewer than thirty seconds to your styling time to wipe the equipment clean when you're done using it. For safety's sake, just turn the thing off and unplug it when you do this. It will still be hot, but at least it won't be conducting electricity. Plus, it's a good practice to unplug things when they're not in use, though I expect none of us are particularly good at remembering to do this.

One final word on cleaning your flat or curling irons: if you find that you have major buildup in need of treating you can make a paste out of baking soda and water and apply to the dirty area, use a soft-bristled toothbrush to scrub, then use your microfiber cloth to clean the baking soda paste off the iron.

Hot Rollers

Do you guys use hot rollers? I really like my hot rollers, and I'm not particularly big on doing my hair. Which actually might be a lot of why I like them so much—they're pretty much the lazy gal's hot-hairstyling tool.

Almost equally as lazy is the method for cleaning them. The first thing you want to do, if they're not already hot, is to warm up your rollers and then unplug the unit. If they're already hot, unplug the unit and let them cool a bit. Then, with a damp cloth, wipe down each roller, being careful how you handle them so as not to burn your precious hands.

If there's still buildup on the rollers, pour a small amount of rubbing alcohol onto your damp rag and give the rollers another going-over in the same fashion. If the buildup is *really* bad, go on and make a baking soda paste and give the rollers a good scrubbing with a soft-bristled toothbrush, just the way you did with your flat or curling iron. For this, let the rollers cool completely, though, because you'll want to have a good grip on them, and if they're hot you might scorch yourself, and no, no, we don't need that. Then rinse the rollers with water, dry thoroughly, and place back in the heating unit.

Velcro Rollers

I'm old enough that I had a Rachel haircut in the '90s. Which meant that I also had velcro rollers, because that's how you styled a Rachel. And, uch, were those things ever a disgusting pain in the tush. There was always hair all stuck up in 'em and yuck, yuck, yuck. The good news, for those of you still using velcro rollers to do your 'do, is that they're super simple to clean. Just rub them against each other (kinky!) to pull out stuck hair, or follow the tips for cleaning a round brush and cut any stuck-in hair out of the rollers. Once they're clean of hair, you can wash them in warm water with a small bit of dish soap or baby shampoo, place on a towel, and allow to air-dry.

Hot Combs

The hot comb is another tool that's largely fallen out of favor but that enough people are still using that it's worth giving 'em a quick mention here. Hot combs, in particular, really work best when they're properly clean, and the design of a hot comb unhelpfully also hides buildup more so than other heated styling instruments. The good news is that cleaning a hot comb is pretty darn easy: fill a medium-size bowl with warm water, add a few tablespoons of baking soda, and swirl it around to dissolve, then immerse the tines of the hot comb (but not the entire unit, which should be cold and unplugged) into the solution. Let it soak for an hour or so, rinse under clean running water and dry thoroughly with a clean towel or cloth.

Hair Dryers

But what of hair dryers? Did you think I'd forgotten about the granddaddy of styling tools? Perish the thought, you silly thing!

Right, but before we get into how to clean a hair dryer, first I'm going to yell at you. Ready? YOU MUST UNPLUG THE HAIR DRYER BEFORE YOU CLEAN IT. I REPEAT: YOU MUST (MUST, MUST, MUST) UNPLUG THE HAIR DRYER BEFORE YOU CLEAN IT.

Did everyone hear that? Okay, good. (But just in case, I'll probably yell that at you a few more times before we're done here.)

Let's start with the easiest part to clean: the exterior of the unit. It's pretty simple, really—just wipe it down with a damp cloth. (DAMP, NOT WET.) (ALSO, DID YOU UN-PLUG IT FIRST??) That will be enough to clean any hair-styling product buildup and dust that may have accumulated. Also, since I can see some of you side-eyeing me as if to ask, "Are you actually serious that I need to clean the outside of my *hair dryer*? Isn't it enough that I manage to dry my hair on a semiregular basis?" I should also add that the hair dryer is also picking up whatever germs and filth are on your hands. And I'll just leave it at that because I think you know what I'm implying is all over that handle. (Hint: I mean poop.) Generally, it's not necessary to use a cleaning product to wipe down the exterior of your hair dryer, but if you're worried about germs—and who wouldn't be after that last parenthetical—you can spritz a small amount of white vinegar on your cloth, which will serve to disinfect any germies lurking about.

Moving on to the innards!

Most hair dryers are designed in such a way that the back grille can be opened or removed entirely (mine twists off, for example)—right, and by "the back grille" we're talking about the plastic and mesh part that if you look through you can see is covering the fan blades of the dryer. Once you've opened or removed the grille, you can use a child's toothbrush or other small cleaning brush to clean out any dust, hair, other debris lurking inside that we'll not spend any more time than necessary contemplating because yick.

If you want to go further and clean the inside of your hair dryer, you can unscrew its cover, which will allow you to get at the components inside the unit. You might need a teeny tiny screwdriver for this; those little glasses repair kits will have what you need. (Those things are absurdly useful!) To clean the parts, you can either use your wee toothbrush or you could get wild and whip out your canned air to remove whatever dust might be lurking around on the fan and motor. Just be sure to be extra super extra gentle when doing this so you don't ding any of the parts—oh, and also try not to remove any parts while you're at it. The hair dryer, it needs its parts, okay? Okay!

Hair Dye Disasters

Home-dyeing your hair is a great way to save time and money while still maintaining your gorgeous color, but it can get awfully messy—especially if you use one of the darker shades. If that dye gets on stuff, oof. It's NO FUN trying to get it up. But it can be done, though in the most extreme cases it might take more than one pass at the stain. Fair warning!

The Bathroom Looks Like Carrie's Prom

Is there a good way of getting red hair dye out of various bathroom surfaces? No matter how vigilant I am, I will always find a missed splotch somewhere the next day, by which point it has had oodles of time to stain and won't come off. After a few rounds of this, I start to worry about looking axe-murdery and gross. Is there a trick or will I just have to start dyeing my hair on the roof/covered in newspapers?

Oh, lady, have you ever come to the right person! I've been dyeing my hair red for twenty years. TEN YEARS, I MEAN TEN YEARS.

I know your question is specifically about the one spot that you manage to miss every single time, but first let me say: I do a ton of prep before coloring my hair. I have Soft Scrub on hand—though here you can use any cleaner with bleach in it. I like Soft Scrub because it's got a mild abrasive in it that gets into the porous material of my bathroom sink without scratching it. I also have a damp sponge, and I line the countertop with a layer of paper towels on which to set my coloring utensils. As soon as the headful of dye is applied, I eyeball every surface for splotches of red goo.

That said, there is always that one damn splat of dye that gets missed, giving it plenty of time to become one with your bathroom. If the stain is on the wall or another non-tile/porcelain surface, a Magic Eraser is your best bet to get it out. For porcelain, a couple of applications of Soft Scrub should take the stain out. To reduce the amount of elbow grease needed, splurt a blurb of the cleanser directly onto the spot and let it sit for ten or so minutes before wiping down. For tile, spray with bleach solution or a bleach-based cleaning product, get at the soiled area with a short-handled scrub brush, and then let the cleaning solution sit for ten to fifteen minutes before rinsing with warm water and your scrub brush.

So that's the drill for getting dye stains off of your bathroom surfaces, but what about getting them off your towels, clothes, and person? Please stay with me!

If you get dye on your clothes or towels and you catch it while the dye is still wet, flush the stain out with cold running water. You may need to rub the fabric against itself to force more dye out, but a good amount should come clean just by flushing it with the water. After that, apply a stain pretreatment and try to launder the item as soon as possible.

If the stain sets in, then things become way, way trickier. Before we get into stain-removal products, I think it's worth suggesting that if you're a frequent home dyer, it's worth investing in a towel or two in a dark color (or dedicating an old towel of any color) that exists solely as your hair dye towel. It's what I do, and it's served to keep my regular bath towels free of the oftentimes revolting-looking stains that hair dye can leave behind.

But back to the stain treatments. The thing about dye is that once it's set it's an absolute bitch to get out. If your items are white, you can try bleaching them. But even that may take more than one going-over. There's a product out there, however, that people swear by for dye stains called Super-Clean. I've never had to use it, because of my aforementioned prep method and dedicated hair dye towels, but when something is mentioned over and over again, my ears perk up, and so I'm mentioning it here.

SuperClean is one of those products you'll want to look

for at your local hardware store, or a big-box home improvement store like Home Depot or Lowe's. In terms of using it for laundering, the fine folks at SuperClean offer these comprehensive instructions, which provide three methods for using their product as a laundering agent:

> Option 1: Presoak laundry in sink or bucket with dilution of water and SuperClean; complete laundry as normal.
> Option 2: Spray SuperClean directly on the stain before adding to the wash; complete laundry as normal.
> Option 3: Add one-quarter to one-half cup of Super-Clean right in with the detergent; complete laundry as normal.

Now that we've taken on the care and keeping of all the things you use to get your hair gorgeous, it's time to turn to those things we use to keep the rest of us lookin' good.

Makeup Brushes

With all that hair stuff out of the way, let's turn our attention to the other kinds of brushes: the ones we use for our face! Before we get into cleaning them, a quick tour of the parts that make up a makeup brush.

> *Bristles*: The bristles, sometimes called the hair, can be made of either synthetic or natural fibers.
> *Ferrule*: That's the technical term for the metal part that holds the bristles to the handle.
> *Handle*: The handle is generally made of wood or plastic.

Now that you know what the parts are, the next thing to talk about is the difference between regular cleaning and deep cleaning makeup brushes. We'll start first with regular brush cleaning, which you should aim to do once a week. (That's what the experts recommend, but I'll level with you and say that it's probably unrealistic that most of us are going to do this once a week.) The reasons for regularly cleaning your brushes are pretty simple: bacteria builds up on them, which can cause breakouts. If you're prone to acne breakouts, try establishing a regular brush-cleaning routine for a month or two and see if you notice your skin clearing up! For regular brush cleaning, all you'll need is a small bowl and brush cleanser.

BRUSH CLEANSERS

Many commercial brush cleansers are available; some popular brands include M·A·C and Clinique. Sephora carries a variety of brush-cleaning products, including their house brand.

Or you could make your own! Here's a brush-cleanser recipe for you to try out at home.

Ingredients and Equipment

1 cup distilled water
¼ cup isopropyl alcohol (rubbing alcohol)
½ tablespoon dish soap
½ tablespoon baby shampoo
Medium-size bowl or jar
Spoon
Empty bottle to store solution (12-ounce size or larger)
Funnel (optional)

Instructions

Combine all ingredients and gently mix together.
Using the funnel if you so choose, pour the cleansing mixture into your container.

Regular Cleaning: Powder and Cream Brushes

Into a small bowl, pour just enough brush cleanser for the bristles to soak. Place the bristles of the brush in the solution and allow them to soak; you don't want to swish the brush around, as it will muddy the cleanser. If you muddy your cleanser, you'll only get one brush cleaning out if it, whereas if you just let the brush absorb some of the cleanser, you can use the same bowl to do the rest of your brushes.

You also want to be mindful of not getting the part where the ferrule and the handle meet wet, which can cause the wood handle to rot, crack, peel, or fall apart. Right. So don't do that!

Once the bristles have absorbed some of the cleanser remove it from the bowl and wipe the brush back and forth on a paper towel—here you'll want to be careful to use a back-and-forth motion as opposed to a circular motion, which will damage the bristles. So think "paint the fence" rather than "wax on, wax off"—getting off as much as you can. If the brush doesn't come entirely clean on the first pass, dip it back into the brush cleanser and repeat the "paint the fence" routine until it comes clean.

The final step is to dry the brush flat so moisture doesn't seep down through the ferrule and into the handle. Lay the brushes out on a clean towel and reshape the bristles if necessary.

For bigger brushes, use a spray bottle rather than a dish so as not to waste the cleanser, because otherwise it will soak up too much.

Regular Cleaning: Lipstick or Liner Brushes

Because lipstick and lip liners are wax-based, as are some eyeliner products, you'll want to clean those last, after you've done your powder and cream brushes. You'll follow the exact same technique; the only difference is that you should add a drop of olive oil into the cleanser. The oil will help to break down the wax.

Deep Cleaning All Types of Makeup Brushes

Deep cleaning makeup brushes is pretty simple and should be done once a month, though again you can use some judgment on this. Maybe once a quarter is more realistic? There's some leeway here, is what I'm getting at. Essentially you're just going to give your bristles a shampooing.

So! Run your brush under warm water, being careful to keep the ferrule and handle out of the stream so that only the bristles are getting wet. Next you'll want to put a drop of baby shampoo or dish soap—here I recommend Palmolive—on a damp sponge or into the palm of your hand. Then, using the same paint-the-fence motion from the regular cleaning method, brush the bristles back and forth until all the lurking residue comes out.

Rinse the bristles well with warm water, wipe on a towel to remove some of the moisture, and then lay the brush flat to dry completely, reshaping the bristles if needed. When the brush is entirely dry you can fluff the bristles back up by brushing them against your palm.

Washing Makeup Sponges

Fill your sink or a small bowl with warm water, add a dime-size amount of dish soap and stir to make sudsy. Then you'll swish the sponges around, squeezing the sponges while submerged in the solution to help get as much of the makeup out as possible.

Once you've gotten your sponge clean, drain the sink and rinse the sponges well, being extra careful that no soap is left in them before drying. If they're not completely rinsed of soap, your face may break out or otherwise become irritated by the residual soap. Air-dry the sponges on a towel, making sure that they are completely dry before using them again.

Eye and Lip Pencil Sharpeners

Oftentimes the sharpeners we use for our eye and lip pencils get gunked up and need to be cleaned out. It's also a good idea to do this somewhat regularly even if they don't have buildup, since you run the risk of transferring any germs lurking on the pencils to the sharpener and creating a bacterial feedback loop. And no one wants that! To clean the sharpeners, just swab with a cotton ball or Q-tip that you've dipped in rubbing alcohol. Or you could toss 'em in your dishwasher, if you're lucky enough to have one. Seriously!

Makeup Spills and Stains

Who among us hasn't suffered from a makeup spill on our favorite dress? Or pulled a shirt over our head only to see that a giant foundation smudge is adding its own version of fashionable flair to the neckline? We should basically just stop wearing makeup. Imagine the time and money we'd save if we went without! (Okay, I'm totally kidding. I basically don't leave the house without my face on.)

My go-to for foundation, powder, and/or liquid blusher stains is to grab a washcloth or (clean!) sponge, wet it, put a small blurt of liquid soap—any sort will do, baby shampoo, hand soap, dish soap, whatever's most convenient—on it and squeeze until it's sudsy and damp before rubbing gently at the stain, being careful to not grind it further into the garment. Lipstick and mascara stains are trickier because those products are heavily oil-based; try a solvent like Shout, Lestoil, or Pine-Sol (really!) as a spot treatment before laundering.

But what about those smudges you get when pulling an item of clothing on or off over your head? For those, I love a baby wipe. Baby wipes are low moisture, so they're good on delicate fabrics, and they contain a bit of cleanser in them, which helps to remove staining.

Sometimes things are a bit trickier, as in the case of this poor lass:

When Makeup Attacks

My pressed powder cracked, and when I opened my compact, some of it spilled on a BEAUTIFUL white silk dress. I don't know what to do—I'm planning to wear it and don't have time to get it dry cleaned. Any advice???

Eeesh, this is a pretty tricky one. Your best bet is to grab a white towel (it must be white) and get it ever-so-slightly damp—like, wet it, wring it out, and then let it sit for fifteen minutes to dry even more. The thing with silk is that it generally hates water, which is one of the reasons why it's such a pill to clean. It's utterly maddening. Once your clean towel is not-very-at-all damp, gently blot at the stain; don't rub, just blot, blot, blot, blot, blot until you think you cannot blot anymore. It may take time and patience, but the stain will come out.

Finally, sometimes people write to me to tell me about miracle solutions to makeup-stain issues, which is so great. This is one of my favorites, and I'm so excited to get to share it!

The Old "Lipstick on the Collar" Routine

I got a crimson red greasy lipstick stain on an off-white cotton blazer that cost a thousand bucks (I know, I know). I thought it was a goner but tried using rubbing alcohol on a cotton ball to see if it would work, and it took the stain completely out! And it was set in for days! One of the greatest cleaning miracles of all time I've ever experienced! Pass it on!!!

How great is that??? And, of course, passing it along I am! Also, please never apologize for owning a $1,000 off-white blazer. That's the kind of thing real women are made of!

Eyelash Curlers and Combs

Just like with pencil sharpeners, it's super important to keep your eyelash curlers and combs clean to ensure good eye health. Ideally, once a week you should be wiping those things down with a clean towel that you've dampened with hot water; if there's a lot of caked-on gunk, you can use a baby wipe or rubbing alcohol to achieve a deeper clean.

Skin and Body Care Tools

Much in the same way as with hairstyling equipment, it's fairly common for us to forget that we need to keep the tools we use to manage our skin and bodies clean and free of terrifying bacteria. No one wants terrifying bacteria all up on their skin, right? Well, maybe someone might, but I think we can agree we don't want to know that person and also that that person will not be interested in this book. So! To the learning we go!

Does the Scrubby Thing Need Scrubbing?

*How does one clean the brush head thingy on a Clarisonic
face-scrubby brush? Mine is not worn-out, so I don't want
to replace it, but it is ... um ... biologically questionable
from exposure to warm, damp shower environs. I wasn't
sure about using bleach on something that I put on my face.
Vinegar? Baking soda? Just replace the brush head and I'm
overthinking this?*

This is a great question and once we're done talking about
face scrubbers we'll get into various other things (reusable
razors, pumice stones, those puffer body scrubber thingers
everyone's got hanging from their shower faucet) that we
tend to store in our moist and hostile shower environs. Because guuuuuuuuh. I know most people cast a blind eye on
the amount of fungal matter creeping around their bath
space, but please stop doing that. This is where you go to get
clean! And these are the things you use to get clean! STOP
SHAVING YOUR LEGS WITH MOLD, PEOPLE.

Okay, but back to the matter at hand: the care and keeping of
face scrubby brushes. The manufacturer recommends washing
the brush head and handle (separate of one another, not together) with warm soapy water once a week to help keep residue
buildup at bay. Wipe the handle dry with a towel; the scrubber
attachment can be dried by rubbing the brush head against a
towel for five to ten seconds while the unit is powered on.

A few other things to note: the handle is waterproof, so
immersing it won't be an issue. The charger, however, should
not ever be immersed in water and, just like hair dryers or
curling irons or any other electronic device, you must (MUST,
MUST, MUST) unplug it before cleaning it, which can be
done by wiping it down with a damp cloth.

If the handle has developed any mold or mildew on it, you can use a very small amount of white vinegar or bleach (and by small amount, I really do mean a small amount; dampen a rag or sponge with less than a teaspoon and wipe the unit clean). If the brush attachment has developed cooties, you should replace it, especially since the cost to do so isn't prohibitive. In general, cooties or no, the brush attachment should be replaced every three to four months.

Shower Poufs, Loofahs, and Shower Sponges

I know what you're going to say. You're going to hoot and holler at me that the things you use to clean your limbs aren't dirty! You put soap on them every day! And rinse them off when you're done! That's what you're going to say.

But you're wrong. So, so, so, so, so wrong. Those things, I hate to tell you, are revolting and filthy and revolting. They're harboring an INSANE amount of bacteria, some sorts of which can cause any open wounds to become infected, or can spread conjunctivitis, or, or, or—are you ready for this one? Oh man, I love this one so much—CAN CAUSE BOILS. BOILS. Ladies, I feel confident in saying that none of us, not a single one, cares to have a boil on her precious self.

Have I convinced you yet that you need to clean your personal scrubbers? Yes, I believe I have.

The good news is that they're easy to clean up. You should do this once every two to four weeks, and on this, unlike on makeup brushes and other tools, I'm actually not going to budge on the frequency I'm demanding of you. Boils, remember? Right!

- *Microwave*: wet the pouf/loofah/sponge and microwave for thirty to sixty seconds.

- *Laundry*: wash with a load of laundry on warm or hot, being sure to check that your hot cycle doesn't go above 150 degrees or so, which will cause the plastic to shrivel up like a ShrinkyDink!
- *Dishwasher*: place on the top rack of your dishwasher and run on a regular cycle. Similar to laundering, just be sure that you know how hot your dishwasher gets before selecting a cycle.

You might decide this is all just too much and switch to old-fashioned washcloths. Just remember to regularly launder them!

Reusable Razors

The next time you change the cartridge on your reusable razor, go on and take a look at what the handle of that puppy looks like. How about the area where the blade cartridge goes? Notice anything, um, disgusting in there? I bet you do! Maybe some mold? Maybe some clumps of hair? Are you totally grossed out yet?? Right, then let's get to cleaning your razor!

This method is pretty unscientific, but it works. This is a thing you can do maybe two to four times a year. More if you want! Basically all you want to do is treat it to a nice soaking bath—here you can plug your sink or use a bowl; whatever is easiest on you—in a solution of either water and bleach or water and white vinegar. Both have disinfecting properties, and the option is yours based on what you have around the house and your feelings on bleach versus the less environmentally toxic vinegar.

Soak your razor in the solution for five to ten minutes or

so, then, while it's submerged, get after it with a Dobie pad or soft-bristled toothbrush to release as many of the disgusting things that have built up inside as you can. Then remove it from the solution and bang it against the side of the sink or bowl you're using to release any stubble clumps lurking inside. Then give it one final rinse in hot water, dry it off with a towel, and insert a fresh blade cartridge.

Pumice Stones

You're rubbing these things on your gross feet to descale them. Please don't even TRY to suggest to me that you don't need to clean your pumice stone. *Seriously.*

Okay, also cleaning pumice stones is dumb easy, and there are two equally good ways to do so:

- *Boiling method:* In a small- to medium-size pot, bring four or so cups of water mixed with two tablespoons of bleach or white vinegar to a boil. Put the pumice stone in the water/bleach mixture and allow to boil for ten to fifteen minutes. Remove from the water (you can use a slotted spoon or a set of tongs for this) and allow to air-dry.
- *Hand-washing method*: Lather the pumice stone with dish soap and scrub it with a toothbrush or scrub brush. Rinse thoroughly with hot water and allow to air-dry.

Metal Manicure/Pedicure Tools

If you want to sterilize your metal manicure/pedicure tools, by all means do so! If they're only used by you, this is probably something you'll need to do only once a year or so, but if you share things like cuticle pusher backers (there must be a technical term for those things), nail clippers, and/or metal nail files, you'll need to do this more often. Ideally, these tools should be sterilized before a new user takes over.

The first step is to wash all the tools with dish soap and hot water. If there's anything that's built up on your tools, you may need to use a sponge, scrub brush, or toothbrush to remove it. While you're washing the tools, preheat the oven to 375 degrees.

Dry the tools thoroughly and place on a cookie sheet, leaving a small amount of space between tools (they shouldn't be touching). "Cook" your tools for fifteen minutes, remove them from the oven, and allow them to cool completely before handling.

And then wash the cookie sheet because eeeew your toenail clippers were just on that thing!

Nail Polish Disasters

There was a time in my life where I swear to God I was getting *at least* one "HELP, I SPILLED NAIL POLISH" question a week and, ladies! Let's all be more careful out there, okay? Okay! This is a typical tale of woe, one I love in particular because it's always fun to put the blame on clumsy dudes.

> Help! My boyfriend just kicked a bottle of hot pink nail polish off the coffee table. The neck broke, and nail polish went all over the floor. I mostly was able to wipe it off the sealed hardwood (there's still some pink residue, but it isn't super noticeable), but it splattered onto my nice cream wool rug. I'm scared to use nail polish remover in case it eats through

the fibers or something. Can it be salvaged, or does he have
to stand on a chair in the corner with a rug ruiner sign
around his neck? Is there a way to get the hot pink residue
off the hardwood?

Well, certainly put the sign on him! I mean, I'm never going to object to sign-shaming the menfolk.

While he's busy in the corner Thinking About What He
Did, you can go get yourself some Mötsenböcker's Lift Off
#3. The Mötsenböckers have a whole line of Lift Offs, but #3
is what you want for nail varnish. That will work on both
the rug and the hardwood. The Motsenbocker's site includes
a "Where to Buy" section, but most hardware-type stores
will carry it.

While the question asker specifically wanted to know
about getting nail polish off hardwood, let's take the time to
go over what to do if you have a spill on your clothes, upholstered furniture, or carpeting.

Fabric

If you get nail polish on your clothes or other launderable
fabrics (towels, bedding, throw blankets, etc.), you'll want to
do a couple of things before laundering. First, turn the fabric
inside out, so the interior or backside is facing up, and put it
on a clean rag or on paper towels. Then blot at it with an
acetone-based nail varnish remover. Flush the stain with
cold running water and repeat as necessary until the blotting
stops transferring color to the rag/paper towels.

Once that's done, there will likely still be a residual stain,
which you should treat with a prewash stain remover like
Resolve or Shout. Or really, whatever brand you like! I use

the OxiClean stain stick, for whatever that's worth, though truly, most commercial brands of stain removers work as well as others. After that, just launder as usual, being sure to check that the stain has come out completely before you put the item in the dryer. If it hasn't, give it another hit with your stain stick and launder again.

Upholstery and Carpeting

If you spill nail polish on upholstered furniture or carpeting, the first thing you want to do is to blot up as much excess polish as you can with a clean rag or paper towels, being careful to blot rather than rub at the stain, which will just grind it further into the fibers. Oh, also! You should do this IMMEDI-ATELY. Don't stop to curse your clumsiness, just get moving and blot, blot, blot. There'll be plenty of time to curse yourself later. Though, actually, the hope here is that you won't be cursing yourself but instead patting yourself on the back for being so awesome that you were able to treat a nail varnish spill without experiencing a major freak-out!

Once you've blotted up as much of the spill as you can, it's time to treat the stain. You'll want to have an acetone-based nail polish remover and either rubbing alcohol or hydrogen peroxide on hand for this part of things. First, put a small amount of the acetone on a clean rag and blot at the stain. Keep doing this, re-acetone-ing the rag as necessary until no more color transfers off. If the stain hasn't been completely removed, repeat the same process, using a fresh rag, with hydrogen peroxide or rubbing alcohol. Then with a clean rag or sponge that you've damped with cold water, wipe away the residual hydrogen or alcohol.

The caveat here is that you should test the colorfastness of the fabric or carpet before using acetone, hydrogen peroxide, and/or rubbing alcohol. To do so, apply it to an out-of-sight spot to be sure it doesn't negatively affect the fibers before proceeding to treat the stain.

Beard Trimmers

I can see you all looking at each other sort of half-confused, half-convinced I've done lost my mind. *Jolie,* you're thinking, *this is a chapter on lady business. And sure, some of us suffer from excess hair woes, but beard trimmers? Isn't that a bit out of bounds?* To which I'd respond, *No. Because we're generally not using them for their eponymous purpose, and let's not even beat around the bush (OH, GROAN): we're using them to trim the hair down under.*

So now that I'm done talking to myself like a loon, and we're all clear on why beard trimmers are getting their moment in the lady chapter, let's get to the hows of cleaning 'em.

Most beard trimmers come with a teeny tiny little brush that you're meant to use after you've trimmed yourself up real purty. The little brush will remove any hair stuck to the trimmer, which yuck, yes, let's make sure all strays are removed and disposed of. Then, to sanitize the blade and plastic guards, if you're using them, grab a cotton swab, dip it in a little rubbing alcohol or hydrogen peroxide and give the blade a good going-over. When that's done, wipe the trimmer dry with a clean towel.

But before I let you get to cleaning your trimmer, I also feel like I should remind you that you should *always* read the instruction manual on any new tool before you get to cleaning it, since different manufacturers/electronics have different recommended care methods.

Electric Toothbrushes

Speaking of electronics, how about we talk about cleaning an electric toothbrush! Sure, let's! I feel like at this point I've terrified and grossed you out enough that I don't need to describe the horrors to be found lurking about your electric toothbrush. Fair? Fair. There are two parts to getting your electric toothbrush in good working order, starting first with the brush head and then moving on to the handle and base.

To clean the brush head

First you'll need to remove the brush head from the rest of the unit. Then you'll soak it, bristle side down, for fifteen to twenty minutes in a mixture of one cup hot water and one tablespoon white vinegar. Some people use bleach instead of vinegar, which is okay, but I'm not overly keen on soaking a thing that's going to go in your mouth in bleach. Tooth enamel is such a precious thing! But it's up to you, entirely.

When the brush head is done soaking, rinse it thoroughly under hot water and allow to air-dry.

To clean the unit

For this you can definitely use bleach, though of course you're also welcome to use white vinegar if you so choose. Just be sure to make up a batch of CLEAN solution, rather than using the same solution you just let your brush head soak in.

Dip a clean sponge or cloth in the solution and go over

the entire exterior of the unit. If there's buildup in any crevices, dip a cotton swab in the solution and use it to get into tough-to-reach spots. Then dry with a clean towel, *et voilà*! Your electric toothbrush is all clean and ready to roll.

Mouth Guards and Retainers

While we're on the subject of your gorgeous fangs, this is for real a query I got, complete with a photo illustrating exactly what the moldy retainer in question looks like. It is a glamorous job I have! And because I am a thoughtful and loving person, I'll spare you the photographic evidence and just tell you what I told her.

> *I am very sad. I have this whitening tray mouthguard thing that has MOLD IN IT. If this were a sandwich, I'd throw it out. If this were a surface, I'd bleach the hell out of it. But this is a very expensive tray from my dentist that I hope to put in my mouth again at some point. I am afraid to boil it because I don't want it to lose the shape of my teeth. Is this a lost cause? Bleaching it and putting it in my mouth seems like a thumbs-down idea to me.*

So you're absolutely right to think that bleach and/or boiling is a no-no. Plus, there's an even easier fix for your problem: denture tablets. Put the mouth guard in a tall, narrow container so it will stay submerged, drop a denture tablet in, and cover it with lukewarm water. Let it sit for twenty or so minutes, then rinse and see how much has come off. If it's loosened up a lot, go ahead and brush it with a toothbrush and toothpaste to remove the rest of the mold. If there's still a lot of mold left on the guard, repeat the denture tablet process.

Just to be sure I was giving the best advice possible here, I checked in with a friend of mine who's also a dentist. Here's what Doug Barker, DMD, added to my tips.

> Great advice regarding using denture tablets to clean the bleaching tray. I would just add that all commercial denture cleaners work the same. (In fact, I tell my patients to save a buck or two and get a generic pharmacy brand!) The main active ingredient is sodium bicarbonate, which you know as baking soda. It's a cleaner, acid neutralizer, which combats bacteria, and will help to prevent plaque from forming. So the only addition to your advice I would include would be to brush the retainer with a baking soda toothpaste on the days that they're not getting the full soaking treatment, which will help to cut down on the number of denture tablets she's using.

Super! I love having knowledgeable friends! The last thing to add here is that you'll also want to clean the container in which you store your retainer or mouthguard. Bleach or the dishwasher will be fine for that.

And speaking of denture tablets, do you know? There are a whole bunch of neat things that denture tablets do besides cleaning dentures and/or funky retainers. Which brings me to one of my favorite topics in the cleaning world: all the weird and wonderful unintended uses for various beauty products!

USING BEAUTY ITEMS TO SOLVE YOUR CLEANING CONUNDRUMS

Product Name	Use For
Hairspray	Pen stains (even on suede!): to use, spray the stain with hairspray and allow it to sit but don't let the hairspray dry. Using a paper towel or clean white towel blot at the ink until it comes up.
Nail Polish Remover	Getting Krazy Glue off fabric; test for colorfastness first (and, um, be more careful with the Krazy Glue!).
Denture Tablets	Drop in the bottom of a vase to get stuck-on gunk up from hard-to-reach spots; use as a soaking agent to get your diamonds sparkly.
Hand or Body Lotion	Staticky clothes: rub well into hands and then go over the staticky material; alternately, rub along hosiery to prevent materials from sticking.
Clear Nail Varnish	Paint the inside of costume jewelry to prevent the metal from turning your skin green; use to stop a runner in a pair of panty hose.
Hydrogen Peroxide	Use for stain removal, particularly bloodstains; dampen a cotton ball or swab and use to clean and sanitize a computer keyboard and other electronics.
Isopropyl Alcohol (Rubbing Alcohol)	Dab on red wine–stained fabric to help remove stain; treats ink stains; takes lipstick or gloss smudges off clothes and cups.

I feel like I've forgotten something important here, but we've covered so much together! Your razors and shower scrubber thingers are disinfected and free of lurking boil-causing bacteria, you know how to get nail varnish stains out of everything, and your hairbrushes are cleaner than they've ever been. What in the world have I missed?

Oh, wait, I know what it is!

You look gorgeous, honey. Absolutely gorgeous.

CHAPTER 5

Here Comes the Bride, All Dressed in . . . Oh Dear, What's That on the Bride's Dress?

W ho doesn't love a wedding?!? A lot of people, sure. But those people are probably thinking about throwing or being a part of a wedding; when pressed, most folks will admit that they love *attending* a wedding. Such joy! Such free-flowing booze! Such egregiously and hilariously bad fashion choices!

And, of course, there's always the possibility that something might go terribly, terribly wrong. Deep down, in a place most of us don't like to think about, exists a desire to witness a wedding disaster.

While we could work in hypotheticals (drunken spills on a bridal gown, a muddy hem, etc.), that's not as much fun as hearing actual, literal stories of wedding disasters, now is it? No, it is not! So I rounded up a whole heap of real-life wedding disaster stories of the cleaning variety, and wow-ee, they will *not* disappoint.

But before we get to the part where everything goes

awry, we should start with the most important part of the wedding . . . THE DRESS. While most brides spring for something new to go along with whatever old, borrowed, and blue items they pick up along the way, some go for a more vintage approach. Which probably means a little wedding dress TLC is in order. Even if the dress is new at the beginning of your wedding day, by the end of the night it, too, might require some attention. I'm here to help.

Wedding Dress Restoration Projects: Before and After

Hannah is getting married! She wasn't keen on the notion of buying a wedding dress because, as she put it, "I am not a pretty, pretty princess," and her grandmother offered to let her wear a white linen and lace dress of hers, which was a gift from her father more than fifty years ago. For Hannah, the dress is beautiful and sentimental and, amazingly enough, fits her perfectly; the only problem is that the dress has some yellow stains, some of which clearly come from perspiration and some of which are a mystery. Compounding the problem, her grandmother has a fantasy that all of her many granddaughters will marry in this dress, and as the first wearer and one who's responsible for getting the dress back to a wearable condition, Hannah is extra worried that she'll do something to the dress in the course of restoring it that will render it unwearable, not only for her but also for future brides.

With the wedding about a year away, Hannah has some time to work on the dress, but she is juggling three jobs, making time and money scarce. Given that, she would prefer not to shell out a lot of money to have the dress professionally restored.

Because of its age, we agreed that it would be better to treat the stains gently, even if that meant taking a few passes at cleaning the dress over the course of some weeks.

Since the dress is linen, I thought that looking up instructions for cleaning vintage linens such as napkins would be a good starting point; the women in my family are great collectors of vintage linens, so I've grown up around them and know that they're beautiful but also need special treatment. With that knowledge in hand, the first product I suggested Hannah try out was Engleside Home Care Products' Restoration, which is designed specifically to clean and brighten delicate fabrics.

While there are other inexpensive at-home treatments using salt, white vinegar, and/or lemon juice, Hannah and I decided that for less than $20, the Engleside product would be our first choice, because it would likely be less time-consuming than the other methods.

So how did we do? We did great! But don't take my word for it; here's Hannah herself:

The Engleside product you suggested is amazing! I have a white dress again! And the big stain down the front is gone! The only thing that is still a problem is the pit stains, which, although faded, are still there.

Aha! Now this is the time to bust out some of the other at-home stain removal techniques.

Well, wait, no, first: this is the time to do a victory lap around our respective homes because how cool is it that a relatively inexpensive product more or less saved the day-slash-dress? I love a happy ending.

But back to those stubborn stains: this is where the lemon juice, vinegar, and salt come in. Start by juicing one to two lemons, depending on how big the stain is. Pour or spoon the juice onto the discolored area and heap on about a teaspoon of salt. Gently rub the salt into the fabric and allow it to work its magic for about thirty or so minutes. Then you'll do two rinse cycles: the first one with white vinegar—a half to full cup will do it—and then the second (and maybe a third if there's still a lingering vinegar smell) with warm water. Not hot! Linen doesn't like hot water. *Et voilà!* No more pit stains.

I'll be on the lookout for my invitation.

* * *

But what of postceremony dress salvaging in nondisaster scenarios? Take, for instance, this example from bride Lyndsay, who absolutely did everything right. Because more often than not, the right thing to do is to live and let live!

> *I ditched my original plan to change clothes to attend the postwedding beach bonfire and wandered down to the beach in my dress. After the festivities ended, the dress was full of sand and sea and smelled like a campfire; I'm not sure any amount of cleaning will ever transform it back into the heirloom I thought it might become. But I had a great time and that's good enough for me. That being said, if you have any ideas of how to get sand, sea, and smoke out of a white silk dress, I am all ears. . . .*

First of all, I'm so glad to know Lyndsay had a wonderful time at her wedding, dress be damned! Things are just things, but experiences are what make life worth living.

With that said, a wedding dress is a particularly special thing, and it's completely understandable that she would want to preserve it as an heirloom. It's nice to think that one day you might have a daughter—or heck, even a niece, goddaughter, or family friend—who might like to wear your dress to her own wedding. My cousin had my aunt's wedding dress restyled for her own wedding, and it was such a special thing for her and for her mom. (Meanwhile, I just side-eyed my mom and was like, "Don't even think about it. Your dress has two tons of lace on it, and a dress that looks like a toilet paper cozy isn't exactly my style." But then again, I've always been a willful and independent pain in her tush. She still loves me, though!)

The first thing you'll want to do is to try to take care of the stains. You'll need a space big enough for you to lay the dress out flat; once it's out flat, first brush all the sand off it with a dry cloth. Then, with an ever-so-slightly damp cloth, go over all the stained areas. Just sort of wipe at it; you don't want to grind the sand into the dress; you want to do a sort of sweep-up-and-away motion. It sounds weird, but actually you treat water stains on silk with water (I know, right?), so that will serve to remove both the sand and the water stains. If the sand stains are really stubborn, you can use a very small amount of liquid detergent to help things along (put the detergent on the rag and suds it up, then wring it out so it's only slightly damp).

This might take a little while, but stay with it.

In terms of the smoke smell, once the dress is clean and completely dry, place it in a sealed plastic container or bag with an activated carbon odor absorber. Poof! It will look and smell brand-new.

If it's worth it to you to spend the money to do this, you can also look up local wedding dress preservationist and have the dress professionally cleaned, stuffed, boxed, and sealed for posterity. The cost will run you around $200–$400, though in certain areas it can be as high as $800. If this is something you want to consider, look into preservationists *before* the wedding, so you can get the dress off as soon as you're back from your honeymoon.

Cleaning Wedding Jewelry

Now that your dress is under control, we can turn our attention to your gorgeous wedding jewelry!

Did you get a diamond engagement ring? Or one with another kind of gemstone, maybe? Lucky you! Can I try it on? Don't forget that you have to clean it to keep it sparkling, and that you'll *definitely* want to clean it before the big day. Hard stones like diamonds, rubies, and sapphires can be brightened up with most jewelry cleaners, but there are also many variations on DIY jewelry cleaner.

One of my favorite diamond-cleaning tricks is to employ a denture-cleaning tablet to do the work for you. That will also work on other gemstones. Some other methods are:

- Hot water and vinegar: one part vinegar to three parts water, soak for twelve to twenty-four hours
- Hot water and baking soda: one part baking soda to five parts water, soak eight to twelve hours
- Dish soap and lemon juice: one teaspoon soap to three teaspoons juice, soak five to eight hours
- White toothpaste and an old/soft toothbrush: scrub gently for five to ten minutes, rinse with warm water

After cleaning, dry the jewelry thoroughly with a soft cloth.

One thing you do need to keep in mind is that soft gems like pearls or opals need special treatment. So if a piece of jewelry you're planning to wear at the wedding involves either, take it to be professionally cleaned or clean it yourself using only a soft cloth or chamois. You should never use any kind of soap or acid-based product to clean your pearls or opals, nor should you use anything remotely abrasive—not even a very soft-bristled toothbrush.

If you've got vintage costume jewelry, you can use many of the same solutions but should alter the method to account for the fact that rhinestones and other similar costume jewelry elements shouldn't be exposed to too much water, which can loosen them from their settings. So plan to apply the cleaning solution to a clean rag, and then wipe them off with a damp cloth instead of rinsing them under water. Jewelry cloths, which can be found in department stores, drug stores, jewelry stores, etc. are also a great choice for vintage or costume jewelry cleaning.

Caring for Your Wedding Haul

While we're on the topic of things to do once you're back from your honeymoon, let's sit with a cup of tea in those fancy new china cups you got from an aunt you actually didn't even know existed until it came time to sit with your mom to compile the wedding guest list. Because those fancy new china cups you got from Aunt . . . um, what's her name again? Terry. Right, Aunt Terry. Those cups need to be handled a bit differently from the set of Steely Dan tour mugs your husband brought to the marriage.

Caring for Fine China

First things first: the thinner the china, the greater the risk of breakage. Given that, be cautious and use the common sense we both know you have when deciding whether to wash your good china in the dishwasher. One other important thing to be aware of is that many dishwashing detergents have bleach in them, which may pose a problem if your china is patterned; over time the design can become faded.

If you have hand-painted china, which often takes the form of very fine pottery, it should always be washed by hand. The paint will not do well in a dishwasher.

These are important things to think about when deciding what to register for—and actually, you should consider whether you even want fine china. If caring for it is going to drive you mad, skip it. If, down the line, you decide that you *do* want a good set of china, you can pick one up for a song at auctions and estate sales. Also, think about politely asking some of your older relatives what they plan to do with their sets of china when they, um, move on. Or maybe don't do that because, oof, is that ever morbid. But it's a thing to think about; many ages ago I found myself staring down the barrel of inheriting three sets of china in addition to whatever it was I was going to register for. A fortuitous breakup saved me from a future of hand washing forty-eight place settings, but right. Food for thought!

Once the china is washed, you want to think about how you're storing it. Unlike everyday dishware, you don't want to just stack plates on top of one another, which can cause chipping and scratching. Places like the Container Store have specialty holders made of soft plastic for plates of various sizes, cups, serving pieces, etc. You might want to consider registering for a few sets of those! But if we're being completely honest with each other, they're sort of unnecessary, because coffee filters, yup, the things that cost a dollar for one hundred of 'em, work perfectly well as plate separators. Don't ya just love it??

Fine Crystal

The very first thing to accept about your fine crystal is that inevitably some of it will break. Make up your mind right now that you are not going to get upset when this happens! And also make a mental note that when it does happen, you're going to go straight to Replacements, Ltd., to look up your pattern and order a new glass.

Now on to the care and keeping portion of the lesson. Your good stemware should never go in the dishwasher. Sorry! You've got to wash it by hand; use very hot water, the hotter the better. If your crystal ever gets foggy, you can use vinegar and baking soda or a denture tablet dropped into hot water to help reduce the cloudiness.

When it comes to drying the glassware, place a towel or two down onto the countertop near the sink and place the glasses upside down on it to drip-dry. This will help to lessen the chance of chipping or breakage, especially if you have granite, or another very hard material, countertops. When you're done washing everything, you'll need to towel dry the glasses; you don't want to let them entirely air-dry, which can cause spotting. The best thing to use for drying crystal is an old linen towel; these can be found for not too terribly much money at flea markets or midrange antiques fairs and shops. Flour sack towels, which are much more easily found, are also great for this chore. Think about maybe registering for a stack of them if you're going big on the crystal.

The last thing to know is that you should store your stemware stem side down. Placing the rim of the crystal down can lead to chipping.

Silver

Just like with fine china and crystal, you should think about whether you're willing to put in the time it takes to keep up with silver, because owning silver means polishing silver. I actually LOVE polishing silver, but I'm also some sort of freak outlier when it comes to matters of cleaning, so don't take my word for it. In fairness to me, I often hear from people who share my love of polishing silver; there's something sort of soothing about the process and at the end of it you can absolutely see the fruits of your labor because *OH WOW, SHINY! LOOK AT THAT SHINE, BOB!* (Bob won't care. Bob will be looking for his set of Steely Dan mugs that you wisely packed away with the holiday decorations.)

If you do feel like you're up to the challenge of maintaining a set of silver, by all means you should get some! It's beautiful, and it's really nice to set a lovely table. It's becoming a lost art, and that's rather a shame.

There are, generally, two types of silver polish: cream or liquid (often also referred to as a *dip*). I prefer a cream polish, and recommend either Twinkle because it's good and also because it's called Twinkle, which is fun to say, or Wright's Silver Cream. There's also a store in New Orleans called As You Like It Silver Shop that makes a brand of cream polish that is extraordinarily good. They'll ship it to you; get a few eight-ounce tubs sent to you at a time and stash 'em away. One last note on silver polishes: unless you're absolutely desperate and cannot find anything else, do not use Tarn-X. It eats the silver. If you *do* find yourself with Tarn-X as your only available option, use as little as possible and rinse each section after polishing and before moving on to the next section to reduce the amount of time the polish has contact with the silver.

In terms of your polishing process, when you're ready to get to work, get yourself a rag of some sort—a scrap of old towel or T-shirt will work well here, truly something you don't care about because the tarnish will stain—and the polish of your choice. Dampen the rag, wring it out, and rub it into the cream polish. You don't need a ton of polish, but you also want a good enough amount to work with. The good news is that you can't really hurt things by using too much or too little, so you can find your own way in terms of the amount of polish to use as you go along.

Apply the polish by rubbing your polish-y rag in a circular motion across a small area of your silver. Continue along in this fashion until your little paw starts feeling crampy, and then rinse the polished area under warm water to admire your work! Oooooh, shiny! I know, it's amazing, right?

Using that bit of progress to buoy your spirits, keep moving along until you've covered the entire surface. Once you've done that, rinse with warm water and buff with a dry, clean rag. (Again, here you'll want to use a rag because of the black from tarnish stains.) You can go back and touch up any spots that may be left.

The most important thing you need to know is to *never* use any kind of abrasive tool on silver, because it scratches very, very, very easily. The back of a scrubby sponge, nope. A scrubber brush, nope. If you need a tool to get into crevices, the harshest thing you should ever use is a soft-bristled toothbrush. If you learn nothing else from me, let that be it. Well, that and not mixing bleach and ammonia—but you know that already, right? Right.

One other thing worth pointing out is the effect that certain foodstuffs have on silver. Salt and sulfur will cause tarnishing and may even cause corrosion or pitting. So if you're using silver serving vessels for eggs, mayonnaise-based dishes, or salad dressings, or heavily salted dishes, you should wash those pieces as soon as you can.

When it comes to silver, storage is really important. Tarnishing is caused by chemicals floating around in the air. Given that, the best way to reduce tarnishing is to store silver in as air-free a place as you can find. A silver chest is a thing you might want to think about acquiring! Maybe a kindly relative might spring for one as a wedding gift! Or you can certainly look for one at auctions, antiques stores, eBay, and so on. Silver chests are lined with a tarnish-preventing fabric and have separators for the pieces, which helps to prevent scratching.

If you're not ready to go full in and invest in a silver chest, you can get silver cloth bags. Oftentimes the place settings you've registered for will come in those bags, in which case, SAVE THEM. If not, you can get silver bags and silver cloth at places like the Container Store.

After all this, you may be rethinking putting silver on your registry. That's okay! Because just like with fine china, if you decide later in life that you'd like a set of silver, you can find very reasonably priced vintage silver at auctions. A thing to look out for in particular is old silver plate, because no one wants it anymore and it can be incredibly inexpensive. Some of the pieces you'll find will be gorgeous and quite unusual. One last thing on collecting silver: if the sets are incomplete, you can still build an "assembled" set of twelve, with a little patience, by cruising auction catalogs or going onto Replacements, Ltd., to search for your pattern.

Table Linens

Perhaps you got some beautiful table linens for your wedding, or splurged on a nice tablecloth in honor of the first dinner party you're going to host using your fancy new china, silver, and crystal. What do you mean you're not planning to host a dinner party?! You don't even need to cook, just order pizza and serve it on the good china! Maybe don't tell your mother-in-law I said that, though.

Inevitably someone is going to spill on your tablecloth, and you should prepare for that now. Commit to not being the sort of person who gets upset over an accident. And buy some Cascade. Yes, the dishwasher detergent. Oh, also! It must be the powdered kind. Mix it into a large body of warm to hot water so that it dissolves completely; there's a bit of bleach in Cascade, which, once dissolved, is going to get your linens back to bright, bright white. While your detergent is dissolving, spray the blemished area with your favorite stain treatment. Then put the dirty linens into the Cascade solution and let them soak for thirty minutes up to two hours before rinsing well and allowing to dry.

That technique will also work on stains left behind from melted wax, so if you've included tapers in your fancy meal of pizza-served-on-the-Spode, this is a good thing to know about. The only difference in terms of treatment is the addition of one step at the beginning of the cleanup process: grab an ice cube and hold it on the wax. The wax will freeze and you can pop it right off the fabric. Then you'll treat any residual staining using the Cascade method.

Now, how's about those disaster stories I promised you?

The biggest culprit in the wedding disaster tales I heard was red wine, and honestly? I think the solution is to take the museum approach to open bars and just ban red wine from these events altogether. But in acknowledgment of the fact that most people probably aren't going to do that, let's go through a couple of things you can do—and more important, products you should have tucked away at your wedding reception for when these spills inevitably occur—to treat red wine stains on the fly.

With that, to the stories! They're arranged in order from least to most horrifying because I like a slow burn on my calamitous tales.

My on-again, off-again boyfriend destroyed a really nice vintage silk tie once when he was a groomsman and drunkenly spilled red wine all over the front of it.

If red wine stains are going to happen at a wedding, the best person for one to happen to is a member of the groom's party. Why? Well, the members of the groom's party are the least likely to care about spilling on their tie. *Maybe* the bride's uncle Bertie would care less, but boy, would Auntie Rita be peeved about it.

The other thing is that, in the pantheon of things red wine can stain, ties are actually relatively easy to get cleaned up, especially at weddings, where there is, presumably, food and table settings and such. The thing to do if you spill red wine anywhere basically is to run immediately toward the closest available repository of table salt. Pour the salt all over the stain, like a giant mound of it (but don't rub it in, just heap it on the stain). In the case of ties it's probably best to take the darn thing off you rather than have to hold it flat in your palm while still wearing it. If you're a lady and get red wine on your skirt or pants, just sit down; if it's on your top half, retire politely to the ladies' room and hang around in there, topless, while the salt does its work. Hopefully you've worn a bra! But if you haven't, hey, good for you!

The salt will absorb a goodly amount of the red wine. You will be astonished! It just sucks that wine right up! You might be tempted to talk to the salt about its drinking problem.

On the fly, the salt trick should leave you looking good enough to rejoin the party. If you're a lady and you've taken your blouse off, don't forget to put it back on. Or do! What better way to get that wedding party started?

There will likely be a persistent stain, which you can treat once you're home by mixing equal amounts of water and white vinegar together and applying to the stain using a clean cloth. Don't, however, rub at the stain—you want to sort of dab or blot at it, so as not to grind the stain further into the fabric. Keep on repeating this action as many times as it takes for the stain to come up; just use a clean part of the cloth as you go along so you don't transfer the stain you just lifted back to the fabric.

If, after all this, the stain is still there, get your hands on some rubbing alcohol, apply it to a clean cloth or cotton pad, and apply that to the stain. Put something heavy-ish, like a hardcover book, over it to hold it down and leave it there for thirty or so minutes. That should remove the stain. If it doesn't, either take it to a dry cleaner or give up hope, your choice.

> *I was a bridesmaid at a super lavish wedding out in Sag Harbor around six years ago, and during the speeches, right before the first dance, you know, the one where EVERYONE takes photos, the husband spilled an entire glass of red wine on the bride. We all had to rush to get her cleaned up before the dance began. I think the wedding planner literally poured OxiClean onto her multithousand-dollar dress. The outcome was a barely noticeable pink stain at the bottom of her gown. And I think the professionals were able to get the stain out when they cleaned it after the wedding.*

This is, like, the mother of all red-wine-spills-at-a-wedding stories. Also, I like this one because it comes with its own answer. (Here salt is going to be impractical, given the breadth of the stain. You'd have to use, like, five tubes of Morton's on a stain that size.) And I double dog like this one because the answer is OxiClean, and Oxi is one of my top five favorite cleaning products. Well, yes, *of course* I have a list. Have we not met?

A small tub of OxiClean will run you somewhere in the five-dollar range. A small price to pay for the peace of mind it will bring you, the bride, on your wedding day. Just think about the relief you'll feel when your drunken brand-new husband tosses his drink all over the most expensive outfit you've ever owned, knowing that you've got Oxi on hand to clean up the mess!

Try to think a little bit less about the fact of your drunken brand-new husband who you're now bound to maybe by God and definitely in the eyes of the law.

I heard of a wedding horror story recently where the bride and groom had an outdoor wedding and it started POUR-ING rain. Like, sheets. And there was no backup plan, so they had to have the ceremony outside, in the rain, as everyone got soaked through and mud started creeping up the bride's dress. To make matters worse, they had ONE keg as their source of alcohol, so during the reception the groom had to drive half an hour IN HIS WET TUX to go get another keg, because apparently no one said, "Hey, groom, it's your wedding, so you should probably not have to drive to get booze." I guess not so dirty as it was wet, but still, bad all around.

Gosh, well, that sounds perfectly dreadful for literally everyone involved. I think the lesson here is more about hedging your bets than it is about cleaning: if you're having an outdoor wedding, have a backup plan in case of rain or, at the very least, a gross of golf umbrellas on hand. And also pick your wedding party better than these folks did, because why in the world was the groom going on a beer run at his own wedding?

Also: have more than one keg. Come on! It's a wedding. You only (hopefully) get one of those; splurge on an extra keg or two.

Okay, but the mud! Who among us hasn't gotten muddy at least once in our lives? It's a funny thing, mud. Most things that cause the worst sort of staining demand that you treat them straightaway; mud prefers that you let it chill, have a beer, watch some hockey, and dry out.

See, the thing about mud is that once it's dry, it's just dirt. And you can brush dirt clear away. Isn't that too stupidly easy for words? There might (probably) be some residual staining, which can be tackled by using a stain-pretreating product like Shout or Resolve and then laundering as usual, or in the case of fabrics that can't be laundered, getting after the stain with a clean sponge and a small amount of dish soap or mild laundry detergent will go a long way. There's also dry cleaning as an option.

If, however, you find yourself out and about sporting wet mud and don't have time to let it dry before cleaning it, grab some clean towels or rags and try to sop up as much of the mud as you can with them. Just do your best not to grind the mud further into the fabric. Once you've gotten up as much mud as you can, go back over the stain with a sponge and some soap.

OH CINDERELLA, YOUR SHOES!

A wedding can be hell on a pair of shoes—especially if there's an outdoor ceremony or reception involved. If, postwedding, you find yourself with mud on the heels of your shoes, wait for it to dry and then rub it off with a dry, clean cloth. Preferably one that you don't mind getting filled up with soil.

If you've worn fabric shoes that have gotten stained, try dampening a sponge and rubbing a small amount of dishwashing soap into it and give the shoes a once-over with it. You want to make sure you work the soap into the sponge, rather than applying straight soap to them, and also make sure the sponge is damp rather than sopping wet. You'll be amazed at how much grime and staining a little dish soap can get up!

Finally, I can't let you all out of here without regaling you with a brief primer on shoe shining. There are a number of good reasons to polish your shoes, the first of which is that it just makes them look better. Regular polishing will also extend their life span, which is a thing I think we can all get behind considering how much money some of us spend on our shoes. The last good reason is that it's really incredibly easy and takes very little time.

Go on and get yourself a standard shoe polish and apply it using a cloth—old socks or T-shirts are great for this purpose—and then buff it out with a brush. There are also instant shine products available, which are applied with a sponge applicator attached to the bottle of polish. Instant shine products don't require buffing or brushing, but you should know that you'll pay a price for the shortcut in that liquid polishes can have a drying effect on leather over the long term.

About an hour before my wedding, the wedding cake toppled over from a table it was set on and fell on the floor. It had been put on a side table that overtipped. I was standing across the room and remember the whole thing happening in slow motion. I think the cleaning was: picking off any carpet fuzz and strategic redistribution of flowers.

It's pretty gratuitous to include this, but include it I will mostly for the disaster factor of picturing the bride watching the most expensive pastry she's ever bought (do you yet sense a theme here? Oh, Wedding Industrial Complex, how vexing you are) go toppling to the floor before anyone even had a chance to taste it.

But also! For those of you who are planning a wedding or haven't gotten married yet but may one day, isn't it so nice to know that even the cake falling clear onto the floor is a thing that can be fixed? Yes! Yes it is.

And this also gives me an excuse to share cleaning tips for getting frosting out of carpet, *which I get asked about way more than I feel is normal.* Frosting (or icing, as some people wrongly call it) is another one of those things, like mud, that is actually better to let dry before you try to deal with it. Unless it's got a huge load of food coloring in it, in which case get to the cleaning as soon as possible so the dye doesn't have time to leech into the fibers.

In either case, wet or dry, OxiClean or a spray carpet cleaner like Resolve is your best bet: it will help to take up the crusted-on substance as well as any staining. Just be sure not to grind the frosting into the carpet while you're cleaning it. You want to work in a swiping, blotting sort of way.

> *You know how sometimes you have sex with your boyfriend in the hotel room before his sister's wedding rehearsal? And then you put on your dress and head into the car? And then you realize you sat in some, uhh, leftover semen that was on the bed and it's all on the back of your shimmery green dress? And your boyfriend's mom asks what happened and you say you got it when you were steaming your boyfriend's suit? Of course you know.*

Well, sure.

(Semen stains can be treated with OxiClean. No word

yet on its efficacy in repairing relations with the future mother-in-law who knows *exactly* what that stain is and thinks you're a hussy and blames you for sullying her son, the perfect angel, with your wanton hussy ways.)

I was a bridesmaid in a wedding and the mother of the bride puked all over herself during the reception. She just sort of looked down and it fell out of her face. Then she wiped it with a napkin and kept drinking and calling the bride fat.

Blinks repeatedly

CHAPTER 6

Laundry. Just ... So Much Laundry, You Guys.

There's a lot to say about laundry. There are water temperatures and dryer settings and stains and things that need to be washed in special ways except that you're not really sure what those special ways are and we're going to get into all of that. And then some.

But before we get to the actual laundering, let's review some basics so we can be sure we're all speaking the same language. Starting with our products. I know, you're like, "How much is there to say about detergent, lady?" OH, JUST YOU WAIT.

Laundry Products

So, yes, the first item for discussion in any course on laundering products is detergent. There are two main sorts you'll find out there: powders and liquids. We're also going to talk about other forms of detergent, but let's pick off the biggies first.

Liquid Versus Powdered Detergents

The most important thing to know about the difference between powder and liquid detergents is actually not a difference at all: they both work! They work a little differently, and they shine in different ways, but both forms will get your clothes clean. So if you're fretting that for years you've been waltzing around in filthy rags because you've been using the wrong sort of detergent, I've got good news for you! You can scratch that item right off your list of Things to Worry About and make room for something else, like whether your gym clothes have retained a permanent stench. (They have. But I'm going to help you out with that, so maybe add it to the list in pencil?)

When it comes to actual differences, powdered detergents tend to have a longer shelf life than liquid detergents, which means you can buy a powdered detergent in bulk and not have to worry about it losing its washing power. If you're looking to cut down on cost or packaging, powders are the way to go.

The drawback to powdered detergents, however, are worth considering. They tend not to dissolve as well as liquid detergents, and can leave a chalky residue on clothes, especially when used in a cold water washing situation (the powder dissolves much better in warm or hot water). There are two things you can do to counteract this: (1) dissolve the powder in a half cup of hot or warm water before adding it to the machine; (2) buy a powder specially formulated to work in cold water.

OR . . . you can go with a liquid detergent.

Liquid detergents have two major advantages over powders: (1) they dissolve a whole heck of a lot better, regardless of water temperature; (2) they can be used as a pretreatment for stained items if you don't have a standalone product for that purpose on hand. The drawbacks mostly have to do with packaging—they use much more packaging than do the average powdered detergents (smaller containers, plastic rather than cardboard, those lids, etc.), so if being conscious of the amount of waste you create is important to you, liquids aren't your best choice. The other odd thing about the packaging of most liquid detergents is that the way the caps are designed to be used as a measuring cup leads most people to use far too much detergent in their wash. Which is actually a bad thing! I know, it seems like more soap should equal more clean, but it doesn't—an overabundance of detergent will make your clothes dingier and is also bad for your washing machine. Now, if you aren't actually the owner of your washing machine, you may not give a fig about that latter warning, but perhaps one day you *will* possess a washer of your very own. It's good to have goals!

A good rule of thumb, if you're using a cap for measuring, is to fill it no more than a third to a half of the way up. That half cap, by the way, should only be for heavily soiled items, not just your run-of-the-mill load of laundry. You can, if you want to, get reeeeeeallllly precise about things use a measuring spoon; no joke, one to two tablespoons of detergent is all you'll need!

Detergent Pods

If all of this talk about doling detergent out with measuring spoons has you throwing up your hands and going, "You know what? I think I'll just drop everything off at the Fluff'n'Fold and let them worry about these things!" then I would like to introduce you to the concept of detergent pods.

Pods! They're such fun and yet have historically not been terribly successful in the US market. They are pretty much exactly what they sound like: pods filled with detergent that you throw in your wash and relieve you of the massive amount of anxiety I've just heaped on you regarding the overuse of liquid detergent. These are great for people who have to travel to do their laundry, in that you can just grab one or two (or three or seven, I guess) depending on how many loads you're doing, rather than lugging an entire container of detergent along on your field trip. They're also great for those who are new to laundry in that they take guesswork out of the equation.

At this point you should be thinking, "So why wouldn't *everyone* just use the pods?" Well, I'll tell you! They present a serious hazard to children and pets, in that they're brightly colored and sort of look like fun toys and they're also just about mouth-size, and you see where I'm going with this? Right, of course you do. So it's something to take into consideration if you've got children and/or pets. You could, of course, get rid of the children and/or pets, which would allow you to use pods with impunity and also would mean you'd have a lot less laundry in general. But I understand that some people feel rather attached to those children and/or pets, so if you want to choose a podless, laundry-riddled existence, be my guest.

Soap Nuts

Before we get into our specialty detergents, a quick note about soap nuts. Soap nuts! That's fun to say! Also they're an eco-friendly alternative to commercial detergents, so if that's a thing that's important to you, this is the place you want to be! Another important benefit is that they're exceptionally good for people with hypersensitive skin.

While their size makes them a potential choking hazard

for children and/or pets, they're quite bitter, which would likely deter either type of living thing from keeping them inside their mouths for very long. If they're ingested, they're nontoxic, so you needn't worry about poisoning (though obviously the choking thing is the bigger concern).

Okay, so what the heck are soap nuts? They come from the lychee family; the pulp is used to make soap. It's a good thing to know where they come from—despite the name, they're not nuts, they're actually a fruit. So if you have a nut allergy, you've got no worries here, but if you've got a fruit allergy you may need to be cautious. They can be used for laundry and also to make an all-purpose cleaner. For now, we'll stick to their use in laundry. When you purchase the nuts they'll come with a small muslin bag; put five to six of them in the bag, tie it closed, and toss the bag in the wash.

Here's how they work: they contain a surfactant called saponin that's released when agitated in water. Water temperature makes a difference when using soap nuts: if you're doing a cold water wash, you'll want to use more of the nuts, but they will last longer; if you're doing a warm or hot water wash, you'll need fewer nuts but they won't last as long. You should refer to the usage instructions that come with whatever brand you choose to go with, but generally you can expect to use two nuts per hot water load, and aren't likely to get another go out of them, whereas with a cold water cycle you'll use four nuts but can reuse them up to six more times.

Once the wash is done, you can either remove the bag or you can just toss it right in the dryer along with your clean clothes; the latter will also serve as a bit of a fabric softener, which is a nice value add!

So those are the basics of soap nuts! The last thing to be aware of is when the nuts have been exhausted of their cleaning power: when they start to lose their transparency and turn a sort of grayish color, that's your cue to pitch—or compost!—them.

Stain Treatments

Real talk: having a stain-treatment product is pretty much a nonnegotiable part of your laundry-product repertoire. It took me a long time to accept that, and I've always been real, real big on laundering, so I say that because I think it's a good thing for you to hear. You need a detergent, something to help with getting your fabrics soft and static-free, and a stain pretreatment product. Now you know!

Stain treatments generally come in one of three forms: sprays, sticks, or liquid. I mention that last one because if you don't have a product specifically made for pretreating stains, remember you can use a bit of liquid laundry detergent to spot treat stains.

The most important thing to know about stains is this: get to them immediately. Even if "getting to them immediately" means applying a stain treatment and waiting a few days before laundering. The faster you get to the stain, the likelier it is to come out.

Since we're on the topic of stains, here's the absolute best thing you're going to learn from me: with the exception of mud and ink, almost every single stain will benefit from being flushed with cold water. Hold the stained area taut under a running faucet and let the water pressure do a lot of the work for you. If you have a sponge or towel nearby, that's even better: use it to help push the stain out even more while under the running water. A small amount of soap—dish soap, hand soap, laundry detergent, whatever is close by—will also really help matters. If the stained garment is dry-clean-only and you don't want to risk making things worse, you should point out the stain when you drop the item off with your cleaner so they can spot treat it.

One last SUPER IMPORTANT THING: stain treatment really depends on what the stain is and what it's on. We'll get into different types of stains in a little bit, but I want to prepare you for this hard fact of life.

Bleach

Bleach is wonderful in many ways. It's also an extraordinarily harsh chemical that doesn't play very nicely with undetectable stains like saliva, sweat, or, ummmm, sexual fluids. For those reasons I don't love bleach in laundry. It can, however, be a good thing when used infrequently to brighten up a load of whites.

Bluing

As an alternative to bleach, when it comes to getting whites looking bright and crisp again, I'm so excited to introduce you to my great pal bluing. Bluing sounds exactly like its name implies: it makes things look more blue.

I realize that this might sound crazy! But there's a perfectly not-crazy reason why dyeing whites that have taken on a yellow cast blue makes sense. It's a little science-y, so bear with me: there's a thing known as the subtractive color model of color perception, and in this model, blue and yellow are complementary colors. This means that adding some blue to something yellow will render it neutral, which in the case of things like white sheets, T-shirts, socks, etc., means that the added blue will make the eye see bright white. It's the same reason why old ladies dye their white hair blue. Kinda cool, right? Another great thing about bluing is that it's totally earth-friendly—nontoxic, biodegradable, nonhazardous—unlike bleach. So it's a win-win, really.

Rather than provide instructions here as to how to use bluing, I'm going to tell you to follow the instructions provided with whatever brand of bluing you end up with. The reason for this is that usage varies dramatically from product to product, so I don't what to tell you to use one method and have you ruin your things because you've used the Bluette approach with the Mrs. Stewart's brand. (Those are two popular and commonly found brands, by the way. You may have to search a little bit for bluing since it's an old-fashioned product that's fallen out of favor, which I think is utter malarkey and am doing my best to change it! Bluing! Bluing for everyone!!)

Specialty Detergents

This is where the fun really begins! There are all manner of specialty detergents out there, many designed for specific fabrics. Now, I don't want you to rush out and buy all of these things, because you may not need them. But I do want you to know what they are so you have a good point of reference when you, oh, let's say . . . begin investing in high-end lingerie and want to treat it with all the care and respect it deserves. I say this as someone who trolls the year-end sales at Agent Provocateur so that I can own bras that retail for upward of $250 for which I've paid something like $40.

Generally these kinds of specialty detergents are designed for use with delicates—which is a polite term for your frilly and lacy underpants and brassieres—silk, cashmere, and wool. Many of them work just fine on any and all of those fabrics! Love that! They can also be used in a machine-washing situation or for hand washing.

The products listed vary in price and availability, and you should check out your options and decide what's best for you. Some of them are scented, some are unscented, some are very specific in terms of usage, some are more universal.

Mild Detergents

- Ivory Snow
- Woolite
- Johnson's Baby Shampoo

Lingerie and Silk Care Products

- Tocca Laundry Delicate
- Soak
- LeBlanc Silk & Lingerie Wash
- WinterSilks Spot Out! (for stains)

Cashmere and Wool Detergents

- Eucalan No-Rinse Delicate Wash
- Iris von Arnim Cashmere
- The Laundress Wool and Cashmere Shampoo
- Pure Collection Cashmere Wash
- Tocca Laundry Delicate
- White + Warren Cashmere Care

Fabric Softeners

Fabric softeners do exactly what their name implies: they soften fabrics. Commercial fabric softeners generally come in either liquid form or in sheets. Liquid fabric softener gets added to the wash, and that's all I'm going to tell you about it because I think that liquid fabric softener is the devil's laundry tool. It clogs up machines, which can lead to buildup that will cause staining. Yes, seriously. You can put nonstained clothes in your washer, take them out, and discover that there are spots, usually sort of pinkish/orangish, all over the place. This is a big problem at laundromats, since you can't control what products other people are using. If you notice it happening, you can ask the laundromat attendants to clean the washers by running white vinegar through them. They're probably unlikely to actually bother, but it's worth asking.

Fabric softening sheets go into the dryer, and are a much better choice than liquid softeners as they won't cause any sort of damage or buildup to the machines. They do, however, leave a coating on anything they've been dried with (as does liquid softener, but to a lesser extent), which is not ideal for many fabrics, including and most especially towels. Never, ever, ever use a fabric softener with your towels. The coating it leaves behind will render the towels less absorbent. And that's a bad quality in a towel! So no more fabric softener with your towels. Also with your gym clothes, leggings, tights—anything with a stretchy quality. They don't love fabric softeners.

Before you become too despondent because I've taken away your precious fabric softeners, I have two alternatives to offer you.

The first is white vinegar, a half to full cup of which can be added to your wash cycle and which will serve as a natural fabric softener and deodorizer. How handy is that?! It will not make your clothes smell like vinegar, either, if you're worrying about that.

The other option are dryer balls, which are lightweight rubber balls that you toss into the dryer. They knock around and help to fluff things up. The other great advantage of dryer balls is that they're reusable, unlike dryer sheets, so you won't be adding to your local landfill every time you go to wash your underpants.

Getting to Know Your Washer and Dryer

Once you've seized upon the perfect system of laundry care products—*as if* there could ever be such a thing! One of the great joys in life is the unending combination of wonderful laundering options out there! But then again, *of course* I would say that. With that breadth of knowledge of detergents and softeners and bleaches and bluing and such under your belt (or, more accurately, in your brain)—it's time to start thinking about the machines in which you'll use them.

The first thing you'll need to know is what sort of machine you're working with: top loader, front loader, or high efficiency. So! Some definitions for you.

Top Loader

These are the washing machines with the lids on top that flip upward. They are, most likely, the sort you have if you have a washing machine in your home. Maybe not, though! You'll add the detergent directly into the machine, either before you put the clothes in or on top of them—the former is recommended, but the latter is fine. Actually, if we're going to get really technical about things, which I suppose we should, the optimum approach is to add the detergent as the tub begins to fill up with water, *then* add the clothes. That will ensure that the detergent dissolves completely, which AS YOU WELL KNOW is of the utmost importance. Undissolved laundry detergent is a scourge on the butt of our clean clothes. (Maybe literally?)

Front Loader

These are the ones with the see-through door on the front of the machine that opens outward. There's a compartment, usually on the top of the machine, into which you'll put the detergent. These are almost always the kind you'll find in a laundromat.

High Efficiency

High efficiency, or HE, washers are also front-loading machines that are designed in such a way as to use upward of 50 percent less water per load than traditional washing machines, regardless of style. Which is great! Both for your water bill and for our great green earth. But . . . and there's always a but with these sorts of things: because of their low water usage, you need to use a low-sudsing detergent designed specifically for HE machines. Regular detergents used in an HE machine will cause two things to happen: (1) not actually get your clothes clean! Remember when we talked about overdetergenting? That is a thing that will happen times a bazillion with an HE machine. The other thing that will happen is (2) all that excess sud? (The singular of *suds* is *sud*, right?) It will encourage mold to make a happy home in your washer. Why? Because mold loves soap. (Mold is also, I'm convinced, a deviant pervert. Rubbing up on soap in that way, ugh, stick with your own kind, mold!) ANYway! Because mold loves soap, if you're using a regular detergent it will leave behind excess, undrained suds, and that will provide a lovely buffet for the mold to feed on. So! If you've gone HE, please be sure to buy a detergent that's appropriate for that sort of machine. Soap nuts, which are low-sudsing, are a good choice here.

* * *

Wow, I actually did not know I had that much to say about detergent. And if I'm being honest, I kept things on a more or less basic level; I could go on and on for *days* about detergent. Which makes me worried about this next part, when we talk about wash cycles and water temperature settings. Actually, you know? Let's make this fast and then ditch school to smoke cigarettes and cook up vicious rumors. That will be way more fun.

Here are the basic things you need to know about wash cycles: they vary completely from machine to machine. Some come with water temperature decisions built-in, and some allow you to choose the sort of experience you'd like for your clothes to have separate from the water temperature they're most interested in. This makes this complicated, to say the very least.

Generally speaking, if you're using a machine that gives you control over the water temperature *separate* of the cycle you choose, the "regular cycle" will work just fine, unless you're doing a special load.

Okay, I just heard someone out there whimper, "But . . . but . . . but . . . what constitutes a 'special load,' Jolie?" A special load—and at this point I think we need to acknowledge that the term has taken a turn for the twelve-year-old boy in all of us and sneak an illicit giggle over it. Okay, now we'll resume being grown-ups.

Special loads! These are the things that are perhaps one of the following:

- Delicate!
- Heavily soiled!
- Wool!
- Cashmere!
- Fine cottons!

These are also things that you might want to consider hand washing, a topic that we'll spend a bit of time on later in the chapter. but back to our machines and the process of getting to know them better.

Water Temperature

As for water temperature, in general you want to use cold water for darks and hot or warm water for lights, though increasingly there's a movement toward using cold water for everything. If you're interested in going that route, look for detergents that are formulated for use in a cold water wash cycle, which more and more manufacturers are producing to keep up with interest in reducing energy levels and costs.

In addition to considering water temperature in relation to the color of your launderables, you want to be aware of the fabrics you're washing. If you've got items that are prone to shrinking in hot water, like wool, cashmere, or fine cotton, you should use cold water only.

Dryer Settings

Just like with washing machines, dryer settings vary, though generally less so than washer settings, which will make our work here much easier. In terms of drying time, thirty minutes should do it for a normal-size load of laundry, but every machine is different, and you may need some trial and error to figure out the relative power of the unit you're working with. Bulkier and heavier-weight items will need more drying time. It's also good to know that medium or low settings are best for your darks because of the fading properties of heat.

With that, here are the most commonly found dryer settings and the circumstances under which you should use them.

Tumble Dry

A no-heat dry cycle, good for delicates or items that are prone to shrinking.

Delicate or Low-heat Dry

Best for items with spandex or other forms of elastic, as well as for delicate cotton and wool.

Permanent Press

A medium-heat drying cycle with a cool-down period at the end designed to reduce wrinkling.

Regular

The highest heat setting, best reserved for hearty items like jeans, sheets, and towels. If you have heavyweight items like jeans that you don't want to fade, turning them inside out before washing and drying will help to discourage discoloration from occurring.

Separating Laundry

Whites, Lights, and Darks

There are two reasons to separate your lights from your darks and launder them separately: (1) so that the dark colors don't bleed onto your lighter items and (2) because darks do better in a cold water washing situation, which helps to prevent the colors from fading, while whites tend to like hot water, which will help to keep them really bright white.

Separating by Material

To further complicate matters, you also want to be mindful of the sorts of fabrics that you're washing alongside one another, as some of them don't play very nicely together in the sandbox.

- Towels can be washed with anything cotton—so T-shirts, socks, cotton or flannel PJs, sweats, sheets, and so on are all fair game—but if possible, should be washed on their own. Because they're heavier weight, they'll be a bit rough on items that are punier, which is why if you do want to include other cottons, I'd suggest sticking with things like socks and sweats that you'll care less about developing pills.

- Gym clothes—anything with Lycra or Spandex—cannot stand towels and fleece, so don't mix those things in a washer setting. The lint from towels and fleece will attach itself to the stretchy fabrics and essentially never come out. Which is no fun for anyone involved, except for maybe those hateful towels, who are laughing maniacally as they dominate everything else in your laundry room.

- Hosiery (nylons, tights, leggings, etc.) can be machine laundered, but should be done separately from towels and other lint-heavy items. They should also go into a mesh bag to prevent them from becoming snagged while they tumble around. They can also be dried but should stay in their bag, and a lower heat setting is recommended. In general, though, if you've got the stomach for it, your hosiery is best hand washed. Another thing to note is that darker hose will benefit, color-wise, from the use of a product like Woolite Dark, which will help to prevent fading.

- Delicates (bras, your finer panties, fancy nighties, etc.) should be washed in a mesh lingerie bag using a gentle cycle and shouldn't go in the dryer. If you absolutely must put them in the dryer, keep them in the lingerie bag and use the lowest heat setting available. Actually, all of these things are best washed by hand, but we'll get to that bit shortly. I do realize, however, that it's not always realistic to hand wash things, which is why it's good to know about how to make machine washing work for you under various circumstances.

Laundering Cleaning Rags

If you've got your own washing machine, the issue of laundering rags that you use for cleaning the home is a pretty simple one to negotiate. Just throw them, and some detergent, in the wash on the highest water temperature possible and that's that. But for many people, doing a load of laundry entirely dedicated to cleaning rags isn't realistic, and they're faced with the question of whether it's acceptable to put heavily soiled items in the wash alongside their favorite T-shirt.

I am one of those people. So I'm going to tell you about the solution I've hit upon that works pretty well for me and will hopefully work well for you too.

Before we get into it, I do want to point out that when it comes right down to it, washing cleaning rags along with your clothes isn't the worst thing in the world. Machine washing is pretty serious business, what with its many wash and rinse cycles. Regardless of how grotty something is when it goes in the machine, it will come out clean after the machine has its way with it. However, it's also not the worst thing in the world to wash cleaning rags separate from your clothes, or at least to perform a little bit of triage on them first if you are going to launder them alongside items that aren't rags. There are two reasons for this: (1) those rags you used for cleaning picked up a lot of dirt and grime along the way that's going to get up on your clothes while they're spinning about together and (2) the rags also have whatever cleaning solutions you used lurking about in their fibers. And those will come out in the wash, which isn't such a great thing if any of those products contained either bleach or wax.

Hopefully thinking about those two things will help to convince you to take this alternate route that I've put together, which essentially boils down to treating the cleaning rags to a quick hand washing before putting them in the machine with the rest of your things: plug the kitchen sink, fill it up with SUPER HOT water and a blurt of dishwashing soap, toss those rags in, and swirl to create bubbles/agitate some of the grime out of the towels. Then leave them to soak for a few minutes—I generally use this time to sort my laundry and pull out the detergents and spot treat any stains—before going back in and kind of smooshing the rags while submerged in the water, which will help to release more dirt. Then drain the sink and rinse the rags with clean water. You

don't even need to rinse them that well since they're going
right into the washing machine, you just want to rid them of
loose dirt and excess cleaning products. Wring them out so
they're not sopping, toss them in your laundry heap, and
proceed as you usually would.

Stains

There are two big things I want you to take away from the
discussion of stains we're about to have: (1) get to them immediately and (2) understand the nature of the stain you're
dealing with and respond accordingly.

That second part probably has you hurling yourself to the
ground in a fit, but please get up because I'm going to explain
to you the different kinds of stains you'll encounter and how
to handle them.

The best advice I can give you on the first point is to tell
you that, with the exception of mud and ink, your best bet is
to wet a stain down straightaway; you'll be surprised at how
long a way good old water goes toward treating a fresh stain.
If you have a sponge or terry-cloth towel nearby to really get
at that spot, all the better. Even if trace amounts of the offending substance remain, that quick flushing out of the
stain you just did will go a long way in helping the whole
mess go away when you can finally toss the befouled item
into a washing machine. If you've got a dry-clean-only item
on your hands, and you feel like water won't harm it, go
ahead and flush the stains before pointing out the spot when
you drop the item off with your cleaner so they can treat it.
The sooner the better. This is your mantra, stain-wise: the
sooner the better. The, um, more spotless the sweater? Sure.
Rhymes are fun.

Two other things to be aware of: baby wipes are super fantastic for stains, especially on those aforementioned dry-clean-only items. They're low moisture, so they won't harm delicate materials, and they have just enough soap in them to help greatly in stain removal. Now you know that! The other thing to know is that those stain stick pen thingies are great and actually work and you should have one in every imaginable place. OKAY, FINE, maybe not *every* imaginable place. That might prove uncomfortable.

Now that I've given you that overview, let's talk a bit about various kinds of common stains, starting with a group called protein stains. You will hear me use this term a lot! You should either be very nervous or very excited by that. But here, I'm going to break down that category into individual stain types and then send you on your merry way. The thing to know about protein stains is that all of them really like enzymatic cleaners. Actually I suppose they *hate* enzymatic cleaners, but *we* love them because they make protein stains go away.

Bloodstains

Oh, those blasted bloodstains. For many of us, they come along with bloating, unexplained weeping, and also an intense craving for salt/chocolate/red meat.

But sometimes they have nothing at all to do with that time of the month, and so we're going to run through a comprehensive list of solutions for getting blood out that you can mix and match to your particular need.

Before we get into it I'm going to share a personal story that is so absurd and yet I promise it's totally true. I am a magnet for mosquitos and also horribly allergic to them. For some unknown reason God has decided to smite me by delivering unto my apartment a family of mosquitos who wait until I've turned out the lights to come out of whatever evil lair they reside in by daylight. Once my home is dark, they *get under the covers with me* and proceed to eat me alive. This is, of course, horrible for me, but it became so much more horrible when I woke up one morning and found a bloody mosquito corpse on my brand-new—and by brand-new I mean I'd laundered and put them on my pillows the night before—Lilly Pulitzer pillowcases. Apparently I'd sentenced the beast to a death by slapping while I was sleeping. I tell you this story to impart upon you this piece of advice: in the morning when I discovered the mess on my pillowcase, I yanked it off the pillow, brought it into the kitchen, and ran cold water through the sink faucet into the stain, and POOF! The bug corpse and bloody meal he left behind were gone like that. I let the thing air-dry (though I could have turned a low-heat hair dryer on it if I needed to move fast) and then put it right back on the pillow. BOOM.

I tell you that story because it's kind of funny to imagine me frantically cursing and huffing about over my ruined ("ruined") Lilly Pulitzer pillowcases but also to illustrate the power of flushing stains out with water. Sometimes in our fear of stains and of making them worse we overlook the simplest solution. The one big caveat to this is when you're dealing with either mud or ink stains, which generally don't benefit from being flushed with water. Ink stains will spread, and unless the mud stains are relatively small ones, you're better off letting the mud dry and then brushing away the dry dirt-form substance that's left behind.

In fairness, that was a relatively small bloodstain, so if you find yourself with a larger bloodstain on your hands (or underwear, sheets, towels, pillows, favorite white jeans, etc., etc., etc., ad infinitum), here's what you should know to get those ugly stains out.

The Soap Method

Hand soap, bar soap, dish soap, shampoo, etc., will all work just fine. Apply a generous amount to the stain, rub the fabric together to work up a good lather, and rinse with cold water.

Using Hydrogen Peroxide

Soak the item in a bowl of hydrogen peroxide for fifteen to twenty minutes and then launder on a cold water setting.

The OxiClean Approach

Pretreat the stain with an Oxi product and then launder on a cold water setting.

Meat Tenderizer (No, Really)

Sprinkle the stain with unseasoned meat tenderizer and add enough water to make a paste. Let that sit for thirty or so minutes and then rinse with cold water, and launder as usual. This a particularly good choice for set-in stains.

Spit (It's Difficult for Me to Even Talk About This One)

Your own saliva will take out your own bloodstain. I'm not overly fond of this method mostly because the notion of someone spitting all over the place fills me with dread, but if it sounds like something you want to try out, by all means. . . .

Sweat Stains

We should probably light a nice candle and pour some tea for this part, because the topic of yellowed underarm stains on shirts is one that apparently makes even the sanest person weep and rend their garments in a most dramatic fashion. So before we begin, let's all take a moment to get our emotions in check so we can tackle this problem in a cool, calm, and collected manner.

There is a whole boatload of weird and wonderful ways to treat sweat stains that employ everything from baking soda to crushed-up aspirin. There's also a host of sweat stain removal products with absurd names like PitStop. They are all great options, and we'll talk through them and then finish up with some suggestions as to how you can prevent or at least reduce these sorts of stains from happening in the first place.

But first let's talk a little bit about the science part of why these kinds of stains happen: even though we usually refer to them as "sweat stains," more often than not they're actually being caused by the deodorant/antiperspirant most of us use. The primary active ingredient in most deodorants is alcohol; in antiperspirant the active ingredient is aluminum. However, if you've switched away from antiperspirants, you should be aware that some straight-up deodorants also contain aluminum. The aluminum reacts to sweat, which is a protein, and causes yellowing just in the same way that bleach will cause sweat and other protein stains to appear more yellow. The last science-y thing I want to tell you—and then I promise I'll stop and get back to soap and such—is that cotton, which is obviously a common material on which one might find a sweat stain, is also a protein. So the aluminum in deodorant is reacting not only with your sweat (protein) but also with your shirt itself. Thank you for bearing with me through that excruciating science lesson; as a reward, here are a whole bunch of things you can try to get those stains out.

The Vinegar Approach

Mix one tablespoon of white vinegar into a half cup of water and soak the soiled shirt in that solution for thirty minutes before laundering as usual. If the stains are really bad, you'll want to agitate the shirt while it's in the cleaning solution by rubbing the stained area against itself. That latter bit of advice applies across the board, actually.

The Oxi Technique

By now you know that I love OxiClean in a deeply unnatural way. If you promise not to slap a scarlet *A* on me for being some sort of sexual deviant, I'll admit that sometimes I whisper sweet nothings to my bucket of Oxi. So it will surprise you not to learn that I consider Oxi to be one of the best products out there when it comes to getting ugly yellow pit stains out from shirts. But a curious thing happened when I started recommending it to people for this purpose: some would come back to let me know that the Oxi didn't do a thing to help cure their pit stains, while others were practically rapturous describing the miracle visited unto their white T-shirts. Because I heard both of these refrains often enough, I put no small amount of thought into this bizarre disparity, and I'm pretty sure I know wherein lies the problem.

My theory is this: the people for whom Oxi didn't work were just adding a scoop of the stuff to the wash, expecting that everything would come out looking brand-new. That's just not the way that stain treatment works, so we have to be a bit more aggressive and strategic in our applications of Oxi.

To really get the most out of your Oxi, it's best to use it as a paste or soaking agent. The powder form of Oxi dissolves best in warm or hot water and won't really make a thick,

fully dissolved paste but it will make something that works
well enough that you shouldn't worry too much about the
sort of weird consistency. If you can, though, throw the Oxi
in some water, let it dissolve, and put the stained garment in
for a swim. You'll also want to get in there and agitate things
a bit; I find that with heavily soiled items, spending some
time rubbing the fabric against itself to really work the cleaning solution in and the gunky substances out is the way to go.

The Hydrogen Peroxide and Baking Soda Method

This is one that comes from a reader of mine, which are always my favorite kind of tips. I love old folk remedies and
such. We should all look into being a little bit more old-
fashioned! The recipe she gave me goes like this:

1. Take one part water, one part hydrogen peroxide, and
    one part baking soda.
2. Mix into a paste and spoon out onto sweat stains.
3. Use your fingers to work the paste into the shirts.
4. Wash on cold, then tumble dry.

She swears (and I believe her!) that this method will take
out the oldest and yellowest of stains.

Preventative Measures

Sometimes we forget to consider options that have fallen out
of style or general favor, but a lot of times they work and are
well worth thinking of when faced with sartorial problems
like embarrassing sweat or static cling or visible panty lines.
I mention those last two because some of the things I'll mention here can also help with those things!

First up, let's talk a bit about dress shields. These are

terribly old-fashioned and yet? They still work. They may take a bit of getting used to, and can't be used with anything sleeveless, but if you suffer from sweating through the underarms of your shirts you may want to consider giving 'em a whirl. Because they're not as popular as they used to be, they can be a bit hard to find, but some common sources are the notions section of fabric stores and the older, regional department stores that are sadly closing at all too fast a clip. Two brands you could seek out online are Kleinerts and Hollywood Fashion Secrets, both of which offer dress shields.

While this isn't specific to underarm sweat stains, it's worth taking a little detour here to talk about slips. Slips! Man, I love a slip. But it took me a long time to get to a point where I was comfortable admitting such an unfashionable thing because my poor beloved slips have taken a reputational beating. Those of us who are under, oh, let's say . . . fifty are likely to consider them things that our grandmothers wear. Which may be true! But that doesn't mean our grandmothers don't have an excellent point to make. I wear mine under summer dresses because my back tends to get a little sweaty and the slip keeps the sweat from going through the sundresses and actually keeps me feeling cooler—and more confident—even though I know that sounds nuts. Slips are also wonderful in the winter when the combo of tights or hose and our heavier-weight dresses and skirts spells static-cling disaster.

Grease Stains

We covered grease stains when we talked about walls and other immovable objects, and now it's time to talk about what to do when salad oil, butter, greasy makeup like mascara or lipstick, and on and on and on and on gets on your clothes. We'll also detour a bit to talk about getting grease stains out of leather and other items that you can't launder.

Just like with walls, dish soap or a product like Simple Green are great choices of weaponry when heading into battle with a grease stain. They are, however, far more effective when used on a fresher stain, though you should certainly not let that deter you from giving 'em a whirl on a stain that's been sitting for a while. Also: why have you let that stain sit for so long? It's terrible how you don't listen to me when I try to tell you things!

Your next line of defense is what Martha Stewart will tell you are mineral oils. Please raise your hand if the term *mineral oils* carries absolutely no meaning for you. Also please raise your hand if you're excited that we've finally gotten to the Martha-shaming portion of the proceedings. God bless, I love that woman but she can be terribly obtuse at times. Usually at the precise time when one is hungover and just wants to know how to get the red wine vomit stains out of the carpet. (I'll get to that, don't worry. In the meantime, go on and take a Tylenol and have a glass of seltzer water; you'll feel better.)

What people like Martha mean by *mineral oils* are products like Lestoil and Pine-Sol. Yup, Pine-Sol. The one thing to note about using these products for pretreating stains is that they may cause discoloration on noncolorfast fabrics, so do a test in an unobtrusive spot if you're at all suspicious that the shirt you've just bathed in salad dressing might not be colorfast. Once you've used those products to pretreat the stain, you should launder the items as usual, using cold water. Also please be sure to check that the stain is out before you put it in the dryer, because once it's been through the dryer it's pretty much set in there for life. YOU'VE BEEN WARNED.

If the grease stain is particularly egregious, like the sort caused by a bicycle chain or motor oil, or if you've dried it and want to attempt one last ditch effort at salvaging whatever it is that you've blemished, there's a product called Mötsenböcker's Lift Off #2, which is formulated for removing tough grease stains. Actually, while I have your attention on the subject of Mötsenböcker's, that's a name I want you to remember. (If it already sounds familiar, it might be because we talked about Lift Off #3 back in chapter 4.) The products are great, and they offer five formulas designed to treat different problems. Another brand name I want you to know about along the lines of Mötsenböcker's is Stain Devils, which are produced by a company called Carbona. There are nine different Stain Devils, and they come in small bottles, so even people who are space challenged when it comes to housing multiple cleaning products can stash them comfortably away for when disasters occur. Mötsenböcker's products can be found in hardware and home-improvement stores, as well as on sites like amazon.com, and the Carbona products are available in those places too, as well as in the cleaning-products aisle of many grocery stores.

But back to that Mötsenböcker stuff: to use it, spray it on the stain, and let it sit for thirty seconds before blotting the spray up. Once you've blotted it up, give the treated area a quick going-over with a sponge or rag and a small amount of dish soap and then launder the item in cold water.

If you find yourself with a grease stain on something that can't be washed, like leather, suede, silk, wood, I don't know, whatever, this is a super thing to know about: talcum powder, cornstarch, cornmeal, and/or chalk will all pull grease stains out of nonlaunderable items. They'll also work on launderable items too—perhaps it's important to mention that!

To use any one of those things, sprinkle liberally on the stain—you'll want to have whatever item you're working with lying flat in order to do this—and leave it for a few hours up to overnight. Because of their absorbent qualities, they'll pull the grease out; think of how pressed powder is used to control oil on your face. Same principle. I know, isn't that such a neat and also kind of gross way to think about things?? Once you let whichever powder you've chosen do its work, you'll go back and brush it away with a dry rag. If there's still a residual stain, go ahead and put a fresh application on and repeat the process. Your patience will go a long way.

Ink Stains

Ink stains are tricky ones in that treating them with too much water can cause it to spread even further into and across the fabric they've gotten into. Rubbing alcohol is the best treatment for ink stains; to use it, apply it to a dry cloth and blot at the stain until it comes up. Be careful to *blot*, though; rubbing at the stain will drive it further into the fabric.

Tannin Stains

Tannin stains generally refer to coffee or tea stains. While they're plenty common and cause no small amount of annoyance to people, tannin stains are fairly easily treated with plain old water. Putting the stained area of the garment directly under a running stream of cold water will flush the stain out; any stubborn areas can be treated with whatever kind of soap you can get your hands on. Put a small blurt of soap on the stain and rub the garment against itself under the running water. Generally, it's best to stick with cold water when dealing with stains so that you don't run the risk of hot water setting a stain in.

Negotiating the Tricky Task of Cleaning Oversize or Nonlaunderable Items

The Bedding

Will it make everyone feel better if I admit that I find washing my bedding, excluding my linens, to be a giant pain in the tush? I know I have to do it, because I am a Clean Person, but I also am forever annoyed at this fact of life. I think it's fair and good to admit that, and also to tell you that even though you can't see me do it, I give my pillows, mattress pad, duvet, etc., the *major* stink-eye when I can no longer delay their need to be cleaned. It feels so utterly defeating. They're so heavy and unwieldy, you guys.

But they need to be cleaned, and that's a fact of life. "Why???" you may ask. I will tell you. Oh! How about a list?! Yes, a list would be a good way to scare you into taking on this horrible task.

1. They smell. Yes, they do.
2. They're harboring a Duggar-size family of dust mites. Yes, they are.
3. Those stains? Are because you sweat.
4. And also? Because you drool.
5. And also also? Because you have orgasms (YAY!) and they make messes. (BOO!) (But way more YAY than BOO, right?) (RIGHT!)
6. And then also maybe because you bleed.

Now that you're convinced/traumatized (I love it when you get like that), it's time to talk turkey and review the basics of how to deal with these miserably filthy and uncooperative items.

If you're working with a washing machine that can fit these things, fantastic! You can absolutely launder them, provided your machine gives you the space in which to do so. And more important, provided that the item in question can be laundered; check the care tag to be sure. (You certainly didn't rip the care tag off, and if I hear otherwise I'll have to turn you into the authorities. It's right there screaming at you, DO NOT REMOVE UNDER PENALTY OF LAW.) Before you do, however, you're going to need to pretreat any stains your mattress pad, pillows, and/or duvet have picked up along the way— especially since they've been there for God only knows how long. Given the nature of most of the stains our bedding is treated to, you'll want to use an enzymatic stain-removal product like OxiClean. Steer clear of bleach, which will cause protein stains like sweat and blood and *other fluids commonly found in bed situations* to become more yellow.

Once you've applied your pretreatments, go on and wash everything using the hottest water setting possible to help kill anything that might be living inside. If you have a choice in these matters you should consider using a gentle-ish cycle. If you've got a top-loading machine, you'll want to put two or three towels in along with the mattress pad/duvet/pillows to help prevent shredding. Maybe throw a laundry booster in to give the stains an extra run for their money? What do you mean, "What's a laundry booster?"?!?!? Get back to the beginning of the chapter. I'll expect a full summary on my desk by tomorrow morning or else you'll be held back a grade in laundry school.

Once everything has been washed, I want you to be prepared for what these things will look like when they come out of the washer. By which I mean: they won't look great. More than likely, unless you're working with some sort of super-duper high-tech microfiber that's impervious to the elements, you'll open up your washer to find a soggy, bedraggled-looking lump that may or may not smell super awesome. But! The drying process will fix that right up. You'll want to use a low to medium setting, which will make for a somewhat long drying time (YOU'VE BEEN WARNED), and a tennis ball, which will bounce around in the dryer to fluff and plump the down filling.

Do you like how I just slipped that in there, like it was nothing? "Oh, sure, a tennis ball. It's a totally normal thing to toss into your dryer!"

Well, actually, it is. Because it's rubber and bouncy and will tumble around friskily with your depressed-looking items, making them feel so loved that they'll perk right back up and become their old fluffy selves again! They're like a rebound boyfriend in that way. And I'm sure if I knew more about tennis and sports in general I would have an excellent *rebound* joke to make here, but alas, I do not. If you don't have a tennis ball handy, you could use a child's small sneaker. Just make sure it's clean of child grime. There are also dryer balls, which are similar in function to the tennis balls and wee sneakers, with admittedly less charm.

Okay, so! That's the basics of machine washing these giant, miserable jerks. And, okay, fine, yes, that's exactly what I hiss at them when I strip them off the bed and prepare them for the wash. "I hate you so much, you giant, miserable jerks." Feel free to do the same! Why not sass the things that give you so much grief? It's not like they can talk back like coworkers or teenagers can. Sass with impunity!

Those of you who don't have washing machines big enough to fit oversize items should come on over for a hug and some suggestions on viable workarounds. My poor little lambs. You can sass too! Sass away!

When you're in a situation where you can't use a washing

machine, the first thing to do is to address the most pressing problem you've got on your hands. So! Returning to our list, let's tackle each potential problem and pick off the solution to each. I think I just mixed my sports metaphors there. Will you ever forgive me? You will, if only because I'm holding the solution to cleaning your stanky gym clothes hostage until the end of this chapter.

Right, then! Back to our list. If your problem is:

1. They smell. Yes, they do.
OR
2. They're harboring a Duggar-size family of dust mites. Yes, they are.

The answer is a steam cleaner! You can rent one of these for about $30, or you can go ahead and do yourself a huge favor and get a clothes steamer, which will also work wonders on upholstery and such. The combination of the heat and the steam will help to drive out both smells and dust mites. A quick note about dust mites: they sound a lot worse than they are. They're also everywhere and you've survived this long without knowing that you've been bedding down with them all these years, so please don't feel too creeped out by this discussion. The main reason to know about them—and why it's not a terrible idea to clean the bedding to get rid of them on a somewhat regular basis—is that they can exacerbate allergies or respiratory problems.

But maybe your problem is one of these:

3. Those stains? Are because you sweat.
4. And also? Because you drool.
5. And also also? Because you have orgasms (YAY!) and they make messes. (BOO!) (But way more YAY than BOO, right?) (RIGHT!)

All those stains are protein stains. Which means that what you'll need to do is spot treat the stains with an enzymatic cleaner. Like OxiClean! (Are you tired of me selling you on OxiClean? I swear I don't know why they haven't yet hired me to replace our dear departed Billy Mays. I mean, I may not have Billy's flair, but I sure do love my OxiClean!) Since the stains are older and you're working them out by hand, you should be prepared to have to put in a little bit of labor to get them up. You know how in the olden times the ladies—and it was always the ladies, grrrr—would work the laundry out on rocks? Right. You don't need rocks, but you do need someone to prepare you for the fact that this task takes some muscle. But you've got muscle! I know you do! I also know that you're pronouncing it like "musk-ell" to make things sound jauntier and therefore way more fun. RIGHT?

Lay your enzymatic cleaner down on the stain and let it sit for fifteen to thirty minutes, checking to see how things are going at periodic intervals. When it looks like—at least, to the best you can tell based on the product you've used— the stain has been hit hard in the family jewels by the cleaning product, go ahead and wipe it away with a clean, damp rag. This is where the fun really starts! Assess your stain. And then get after your stain with that same rag that you've wrung out to rid of all the stuff you just wiped up and your muscles (musk-ells). You might sweat! This is okay! It's work! If there's still staining, go ahead and put a bit more of your enzymatic cleaner on there, and a little laundry detergent or even dish soap, and keep going after the stain with the power of your body. Think a little about the mechanics of a washing machine here: the machine uses soap and water, sure, but the real magic is to be found in the agitating motion of the device. So do your very best to re-create the experience of a washing machine using only the power of your little arms. Bonus: you've gotten out of doing bicep curls for *at least* two days.

There is, however, an important difference between you and a washing machine. Actually there are a number of differences, but for our purposes we're going to focus on only one: you do not have a spin cycle draining mechanism and the washer does. What this means is that you'll want to be aware of not *soaking* the oversize item you're cleaning. Don't use a sopping wet rag for this purpose, do be sure to wring it out. While flushing dirty or stained items with water is ideal, in the case of oversize items that can't be treated to a superfast spin cycle to cast out all that demon water, followed by a tumble in a nice warm dryer, it's going to create more headaches for you because it will basically never dry. And then it will probably start to smell the way things smell when they basically never dry. So! This should be a low-water experience for everyone involved.

When you feel like you've gotten the stain out, wring your rag entirely clean and go over the spot a few times to get up the last of the cleaning products you've used. Then let the thing air-dry for a few hours, check to make sure the stains are out, finally turning a hair dryer on the wet spots to finish off the drying process.

And finally, if your problem is:

6. And then also maybe because you bleed.

There are, as we discussed up-chapter, a whole host of treatments for bloodstains. If you've got one on a mattress, pillow, feather topper, or mattress pad, meat tenderizer is probably your best bet, as it works exceedingly well on older blood stains. The other good thing about meat tenderizer, which you'll make into a paste using water and then use as a spot treatment, is that you can control how much liquid goes into it, which is helpful when treating items that will need to be air-dried (or hair-dried).

To reiterate your basic meat-tenderizer-as-stain-treatment instructions: sprinkle the stain with unseasoned meat tenderizer (the white stuff) and add enough water to make a paste. Let that sit for thirty or so minutes and then rinse with a rag that's been dipped in cold water and wrung out. The same warnings apply about keeping the process as low moisture as possible here, so you may have to go over the area a few times to completely remove the tenderizer paste you made and to work out the stain.

Hand Washing Delicate or Dry-Clean-Only Items

Bras

Before we get into how to hand wash a brassiere, we need to get an important topic our of the way first: yes, you must wash your bras. I'm not going to insist that you wash them by hand, though you should and I'll get into the whys of that shortly, but you have to wash them. Sorry, it's tough love time.

"But," I can hear you starting already with me, "my boobs don't get dirty!" Which, okay, sure. It's not really true, but I've learned not to try to press this point with women who have decided that this is a statement of fact. Rather, the point I will make to you is this: while your boobs may not get dirty (they do), your underarms are full up on sweat, and smells, and chalky white deodorant or slimy clear deodorant unless you eschew deodorant altogether, in which case please see above. Also you cannot tell me that you've never felt a trickle of sweat down your back on a particularly hot summer day. You just cannot even try to get that one past me.

The point here is this, your bra goes over your boobs but also under your armpits and around your back with the trickle of sweat that you and I both know is there. And those areas get dirty, even if your boobs don't. (They do.) Here is another thing to consider: your skin? Is full of oil and that oil excretes onto your bras. Also your skin? It sheds. All over your bras. Let's clarify that point: your bra is full of dead skin. I mean, it's *your* dead skin, but still—dead skin. You're basically molting all over your boulder holder, lady. So! You need to wash your bras!

The best way to wash your brassieres is by hand, as they are delicate flowers that don't care for all the jostling that goes on in a washing machine. It can warp the underwire and stretch out the elastic in the back and shoulder straps. If you absolutely must wash your bras in the machine, here are the things you should know about that process: (1) put the bras in a mesh bag to help protect the straps and hooks from snagging and becoming misshapen; (2) use a gentle detergent designed for delicates; (3) use the delicate cycle on the machine and either cold or warm water; and the most crucial point is (4) never put your bras in the dryer. Allow them to air-dry. Thank you for your attention to this important matter.

Brassiere Maintenance

While this isn't technically cleaning, let's have a quick chat about how we're treating our bras in general. Bras are freaking expensive! So let's make them last as long as possible, yes? Yes! An important thing to keep in mind when it comes to caring for your bras is the importance of rotating your collection. It needn't even be a big collection! Some people have a small number of bras, for various reasons. Regardless of how many bras you're working with, a general rule of thumb is to not wear a bra more than once in a row without giving it a day off to recover from the taxing work of holding your bosoms up all day. Giving a bra a day off will help preserve the integrity of the elastic, which is sensitive to the heat and oils produced by your body. In terms of how often to actually launder your bras, while it largely depends on the size of your collection, for the sake of providing a guideline, washing them every three to six wearings is not a bad standard. You can adjust that as you see fit, but please do keep in mind those bodily oils and the skinsuits your bras are wearing.

Brassiere Hand-Washing Instructions

The best place to do hand washing of any sort, excepting very large items, is in the kitchen sink. The bathtub or bathroom sink will also work. Or a bucket! Essentially what you're looking for is a place where you can create a standing body of water

Do I need to tell you to clean that sink out first? I probably do. Okay, so—please clean the sink (or tub or bucket) first!

Once the sink is clean, plug the drain and begin filling the sink with warm water and a mild detergent of your choosing. As we've discussed with regard to regular old laundry, you don't need or want to use a lot of detergent—a teaspoon will do it. This is especially true when dealing with hand washing and delicate items that will react more dramatically in the face of excess detergent. Be mindful of their feelings, please! Swirl your hand about in the water to help create some suds and then go ahead and put your brassieres into the lovely bubble bath you've drawn for them. Let them enjoy a nice soak for ten or so minutes.

After they've had a chance to let Calgon take them away, you'll want to go in and gently press on each one just a bit, while submerged, to help release dirt and oil and their skin-suits that have become trapped in the fabric. Then drain the wash water and rinse each bra thoroughly with clean water. I generally find it easiest to drain, rinse, replug, and refill the sink with clean water before resubmerging my bras as the first pass in rinsing them.

When you're satisfied that they're fully rinsed of detergent—and that point is important, since leaving soap residue in the bra will also shorten its life span—it's time to dry them. Using your hands, gently squeeze out as much wa-ter as you can, being careful not to wring or otherwise get too rough in your handling of these delicate items. Then lay out a clean towel and place each bra on it, leaving a bit of space between each one so that you can roll the towel up in order to squeeze more water out of each item. The final step is to reshape each bra and allow it to dry either flat or on a drying rack.

Treating Stains

Sometimes stains happen on your bras! (Now will you con-cede that they get dirty? I'm determined to break you on this point.) If any of your clothes ever stain your bras with dye, you'll want to treat them in the same way you would stains on other clothes—you just want to be mindful of the prod-ucts you choose and go for as gentle an option as you can find. OxiClean is a safe choice, though as with detergent you'll want to be sparing with it and, if you're using the pow-dered form, dilute it a bit before applying it to the stains. It will also help to gently rub the fabric against itself to help work the product in and the stain out. Once you've spot treated the befouled area, you can put the bra into the bubble bath with the rest of its friends for a nice swim.

A quick note on deodorant residue/staining: if you use a deodorant that's left behind white residue, you likely don't need a special stain treatment for it—just rub the fabric of the bra against itself while submerged in the sudsy water. Gel-style deodorants may leave behind an oily residue that causes a darkening of the fabric. If that's what you've got going on, you'll want to grab a product that will treat oily stains, like Lestoil or Pine-Sol. Because the items you're cleaning are so delicate, do try to use them sparingly. If you want to elimi-nate deodorant residue in between wearings, you can wipe the stained areas clean with a damp washcloth (a clean sponge or rag or whatever will also work). Don't rub too, too hard, but also don't be afraid to put a little muscle into it.

Silk

Ah, silk, that beautiful and difficult vixen. Dry cleaning is generally the best option when it comes to caring for silk, as the material is so delicate and temperamental. But you can hand wash your silken items, which is a thing that often sur-prises people until it's pointed out that people were wearing silk clothing long before dry cleaning was invented and then they sort of go, "Oh! Yes, I suppose that makes some sense."

So yes, you can wash your silks! But there are a few things to know before you decide if going that route is the best one for you. First, it's entirely likely that the feel of the fabric will change a bit after hand washing; it may become less smooth. Hand washing may also cause the color of the fabric to darken slightly. You'll want to know those things so you can decide if you want to DIY it or send your silken items out to the dry cleaner.

If you *do* decide to hand wash them, here are the things you need to know.

- You'll want to use a detergent specifically made for use on silk and only use a very small amount of it. I know I'm starting to sound like a broken record with all the "only a very small amount of detergent" business, but I can personally attest that breaking the overdetergenting habit is a hard thing to do—it just feels so intuitive that more detergent = better!—so I'm repeating myself in the hopes that you'll remember me nagging at you and work on being mindful of how much detergent you're using. This is for your own good; it hurts me more than it hurts you; I'm not mad, I'm just disappointed; etc.

- Don't soak the item too long; hand washing silk should be a fairly quick process. It's also crucial to maintain a single water temp—either cold or lukewarm—as the silk will react badly to water temperature changes, and keeping a standard water temperature will help to cut down on potential changes to the feel or color of the fabric. Another thing that will help to maintain the look and feel of the fabric is to add a tablespoon of white vinegar to the water, which will help to prevent the silk from taking on a matte finish.

- To dry the items, lay them out flat to air-dry. Once the item is dry, you can use a steamer on a very low setting, held at a safe distance from the item to prevent water spotting, which will help to restore the softness and feel of the item.

- Silk can also be machine washed! I know, this is bordering on crazy talk. The caveat here is, of course, that you need to have a machine that offers a gentle cycle and use cold water only. You should also wash any silkens separate of any nonsilk items.

- You can also put silk in the dryer! But: you can only tumble dry it on a no-heat setting, and truly, letting the items air-dry is much more strongly recommended. Because silk wrinkles so easily, if you need to press a silk item, do so when it's still slightly damp, use the lowest heat setting possible, and turn the item inside out before ironing. Steaming is a better option, generally, when it comes to silk.

Cashmere

Just like with silk items, dry cleaning is the go-to choice for a lot of people when it comes to cleaning cashmere, and while it's a fine—and convenient—option, it's also expensive. Also, hand washing turns out to be a better way to care for your cashmere! If you have a washing machine with a delicate-wash cycle option, you can also wash cashmere that way, but the same rules apply to your sweaters as do to your bras: use a mesh bag, a gentle cycle, cold water only, and a mild detergent made for cashmere.

Technique-wise, the process will look a lot like the one I assigned you for washing your bras: fill the kitchen sink with cold or lukewarm water, add a gentle detergent, place the sweaters in the wash water, and swirl them gently about for three to five minutes. You don't want to wring them, or force running water though the fibers, which can result in stretching. The swirling will help to release some of the oils and skin and dirt from the fabric.

When you're ready to rinse the garments, move them off to the side of the sink so you can drain the dirty water. Then refill the sink with clean water, and give the sweaters another swirl around in the clean water to release the suds from the fibers. In addition to swirling them about, you can give 'em a little smoosh while submerged in the water to press out some suds. Just don't wring or stretch the material; it's delicate stuff! The last step is to drain the sink and give each item one last squish in the empty sink to push out as much water as possible. Then lay the items out flat on a clean towel and roll the towel up, pressing gently to help extract as much moisture as possible. Then unroll the towel and lay the item out flat to air-dry.

Wool

Oh my God, yes, you can also wash wool by hand!!!!! Are you ready to throttle me yet? I'm sorry! It's just that people ask me about all manner of "dry-clean-only" articles of clothing, so I'm trying to cover the most popular material types that folks ask about.

The same caveats apply to wool as to silk and cashmere: hand washing wool and other fine fabrics is generally pretty much fine, but there are some things you'll sacrifice in choosing not to take your "dry-clean only" items to the dry cleaner. Most notably, the fabric may lose some of its softness and may experience a bit of shrinkage and/or color loss. This is particularly true of wool. For that reason, if you do want to try your hand at cleaning your woolens at home, I would suggest you start with hand washing it before experimenting with using the gentle cycle on your washing machine.

If true hand washing goes fine and you're feeling confident, you can absolutely try out the machine version, provided you've got the right settings and only cold water unless you want a new outfit for your favorite dollie (heat + wool = enemies for life), but you should also note that wool doesn't love to be overhandled, and so even using the delicate cycle, the friction caused by the washing machine might leave the fabric looking a little on the shabby side.

Your hand-washing instructions look just like the ones for cashmere: make a bubble bath for your clothes using a small amount of mild detergent, preferably one designed for woolens, and cold water. Lukewarm at the most. We're looking to avoid the creation of doll clothes, remember? Next you'll submerge the garment(s) and let them soak for three to five minutes. Then, while still submerged, gently press/ squeeze it so that the water and detergent can get into the fibers. Just like with cashmere, you are not to wring your wool clothes—it's just way too hard on the fabric. Then, using clean water, you'll rinse the items free of soap, squeezing gently to remove excess water. Squeezing. Not wringing.

Once you've squeezed out as much excess water as you can, lay the garment out flat to dry. With wool, you never want to hang it dry, because wool is quite a heavy fabric and the weight of it will cause the garment to stretch out in ways that you likely don't want it to.

Now, then, one more thing I want to add is that those instructions are best applied to lighter-weight woolen items like dresses, slacks, and sweaters. One issue with washing wool sweaters is that they tend, and this is especially true of heavier-weight ones, to take on a bit of a wet-dog odor when washed, and that they don't dry as quickly as do items like dresses and slacks.

The same thing is true of heavy winter coats. Which brings me to the portion of the discussion where we talk about your winter coats. If you live in a warm-weather climate and do not require the use of winter coats, (1) I hate you and (2) you can skip right over this.

Here is a thing I often hear from people, and the reaction is always the same—a wild clutching of pearls: "Am I supposed to clean my wool winter coat? I never have." I presume that these people think their coats are made of magic and that sometime in June the winter coat that was put away in April miraculously renders itself clean of all the grime it collected during the however many months it was in service. This is, of course, an absurd notion. A lovely one to think about, to be sure, but also absurd and not gonna happen unless you're Harry Potter, and I'm sorry to also have to break more bad news to you, but you're not Harry Potter.

Now that I've traumatized you with the truth about your coats and your lack of wizarding abilities, it's time to come to grips with the fact that your winter coats need to be cleaned at the end of the season. Because they're so heavy, hand washing is really not ideal, and so the thing to do is to brace yourself and your wallet and bring anything wool to the dry cleaner. Yes, it will be costly. But we can put it in a little perspective to help ease the pain: it's an annual expense, not a regular one, and when you consider the cost of a coat, spending $10–$20 a year to maintain it really isn't too terribly much. So from now on, at the end of the colden times, I want you to gather up your coats and march them down to the dry cleaner. If you've got a few coats, you can even ask if you can get a discount on the total cost. The worst they can say is no!

Part of the reason it's important to dry-clean your coats before you put them away for the summer is that any stains on there will set in over the time that they're stashed in storage. Because winter coats are often dark, it can sometimes be hard to see that the stains are even there, but they assuredly are and they'll weaken the fabric as well as just be generally germy and gross.

If your coats aren't stained but have a not-so-fresh smell about them, there are a few great things to know about in terms of eliminating odors in items that you can't just toss in the washing machine. These methods can be applied to items other than just woolen overcoats, and lead us nicely into our discussion of smells and what to do about them.

Smells

Smells are super tricky things because oftentimes they end up on or in or all over things that can't just be easily tossed into a washing machine, and that is one of life's more frustrating realities, isn't it? Fortunately, there are a whole bunch of options out there for getting unwanted scents out of your favorite items.

The Powder Method

There are several powdery things that will help greatly when it comes to pulling unwanted scents out of nonlaunderable items (or items you just don't feel like laundering). Among these are baking soda, which you've likely encountered in your life, but you should also know about Borax for this purpose and also activated charcoal. Activated charcoal, also known as active charcoal or carbon, is a thing I particularly want to chitchat about with you. I love this stuff. It can be found in plant and pet stores, and is also available on amazon.com.

Because these things are powders, here's a quick rundown on how to use them without getting your stanky clothes all dusty. Because dusty *and* stanky clothes are not going to be of any help to anyone. So we need to contain the dust somehow, while still leaving it out and about enough to work its odor-absorbing magic. The best solution I've hit on, which is a bit DIY and therefore so much fun, is to put the item in a plastic garbage or garment bag, or in a sealable storage container, lie it out flat, and insert a bowl filled with whichever product you're going with so that it sits upright. Then seal the bag or container and let the stinking thing hang out for a few days. It will take up a little space, which is a bummer, but I think you'll survive it.

If all of this just seems like too much work for you, I've got one more trick up my sleeve. Actually, I've got loads of tricks up my sleeves, but I think by now you are well aware of that fact. Man, I really love tricks and sleeves. Sorry, what were we talking about? Oh, right, activated charcoal. Okay, this is so freaking great and I'm so freaking excited to tell you about it: there's a company called Innofresh that makes active charcoal odor absorbers in block form, and they are utterly fantastic; everyone I've ever pointed in the direction of the Innofresh line has raved about how well they work. So I want you to know that name and keep it in mind when you end up with something stinky on your hands that you can't just toss in the laundry machine. They are going to be your best friends. I mention this because if you don't have room to seal up and lay flat whatever item you're trying to make smell fresh, these are an awesome option for you: put the item in question on a hanger, hang an odor absorber on the hanger (they come with little hooks!), then put it all inside a garment or trash bag, seal it up, hang it in your closet for two days, and that's that. So easy, right? Right!

The Steam Method

So here's a thing that I sometimes still have a hard time wrapping my mind around, even though I know it to be true: steaming will remove lingering odors from clothes and other items like mattresses. I know! Doesn't that strike you as so odd? The other great thing about using a steam cleaner is that you can add a scent to the water tank—scented linen spray can be used for this, or a drop of essential oil that smells the way you'd like to smell—which will infuse a lovely scent, replacing the old, not-very-lovely one.

The Air Method

Blessedly, we no longer live in medieval times when air was considered the devil and so we can take the saying "air it out" to heart. It is actually true that just letting something air out will go a long way in making it smell fresh and so, if you have a secure outdoor space in which to do so, go on and hang your things outside. Just check the weather report first. If you don't have a secure outdoor space, you can hang the garment in front of or near an open window, as long as doing so won't cause you to suffer from hypothermia.

Now, then, there are some times in life when your smell problems require more than powder, and so it's time to talk about what to do when your clothes or sheets or towels go stanky on you.

Mildewed Laundry

Here's a thing that's assuredly happened to even the best of us: we put in a load of laundry and then . . . promptly forget about it. And when we finally do remember about that load of laundry, we're faced with a soggy, stinking pile of clothes or towels or sheets and also a tangible representation of our own failure to function as an adult. ("I forgot my own laundry. I am a child who is ill equipped to handle the most basic of tasks.") Or maybe that's just me? I certainly hope I'm the only one who's so hard on myself, because I would be so upset to think of you abusing yourself in that way. *Because it's just laundry.* Plus, there's an absurdly easy way to fix the problem. And what could be more grown-up than knowing and employing a solution to a mess that's been made?!

The solution to a pile of mildewed stuff is to rewash it with your regular detergent as well as a cup or two of white vinegar. A note on amounts: for a regular washing, a half cup to a full cup of white vinegar is more than enough to help cut down on smells and serve as a natural fabric softener. But when you're dealing with overpowering smells like mildew, you'll need to up the ante, and being aware of those differences will help you to apply that understanding to various laundering situations you may find on your hands.

Baking soda is another option, but I prefer vinegar because I think it works better, and also because it has that fabric-softening property, which a half-dried pile of laundry that's gotten a bit crunchy from sitting around all wet and miserable will likely benefit from. If you've only got baking soda around, or just prefer it, one way to make it more effective is to soak the mildewed item in the bathtub using hot water and baking soda, before laundering as usual. The one thing you don't want to do is to mix the baking soda and the vinegar, because as much fun as volcanoes are, they're not super in the washing machine.

A related thing that can happen if you leave wet clothes in the washer, is that the washer itself may take on a mildew smell. This also sometimes just happens, regardless of whether you've left clothes hanging around; this is particularly true of front-loading machines, as the rubber seal around the opening of the machine can trap water, which over time will turn to mold and create that mildew smell. If this is the case, your first course of action should be to run two cups of white vinegar through the machine while empty, using the hottest water setting possible. You can also use bleach, but given the choice I would suggest going with the vinegar because you won't run the risk of having any left-behind bleach residue ruin your clothes, and also you won't be dumping a few cups of bleach into our water supply, which is kind of a nice thing.

The last step in this, especially if you've got a front loader, is to take a rag dipped in either vinegar or bleach and wipe down all the rubber seals, being sure to get into their inner folds where water may have collected and gone funky on you. If you've used bleach, it's really important to go back over it a few times with water to rinse away all that residue so it doesn't damage any of your clothes.

Your Gym Clothes Stink Even When They're Clean

Come sit with me for a spell. Would you like a cup of tea or an electrolyte-restoring cold drink? You're probably thirsty after that workout. Oh, sorry, I just assumed you were coming from the gym. Because . . . and, oh boy, this is awkward . . . those gym clothes you're wearing? They smell kinda funky. Even though they're clean, yeah.

Okay, realistically no one is ever going to actually say that to you because it's so, so awkward. But it's extraordinarily common for gym clothes to take on a lingering smell that mere laundering doesn't eliminate. And that's where I come in because I have a TRICK for you. Hurrah! We love tricks!

The trick is also really simple. It involves white vinegar, as do so many of my tricks. So here goes: Woolite Dark + white vinegar (use regular Woolite if you've got light-colored athletic gear), in the kitchen sink with cold water, let your stanky gym clothes soak for thirty minutes (maybe giving the crotchal/underarm areas a little *chh-chh* frottage action), rinse, rinse, rinse, rinse, rinse, press the clothes of water (don't wring! It's bad for the Lycra!) and then air-dry. The vinegar smell will dissipate but will also remove any lingering personal odors.

Oh, also, clean the sink first and, you know, take the dishes out of it?

So . . . remember back when we started this laundering journey together you were all, "How much is there to say about detergent, lady?" They were simpler times, weren't they? Here's the funny thing, though: I bet there are still things you want to know about laundry procedures. And there are more things I want to tell you about laundry procedures! But we've got limited time here and also I am nothing if not a merciful Clean Person, so I'm declaring that laundry school's out for summer.

CHAPTER 7

Pimp Your Ride

You wanna hear a funny thing about me? I love washing a car, but I haven't the foggiest notion as to how to operate one. Strange but true! And even though I don't actually drive, I do have a lot of car freaks in my life and so I'm always asking them to share their little pearls of car-freak wisdom. And now I finally get to share those pearls with people who can actually use them. You know, the kind of people who, like, own a car.

Washing the Car, Part I: The Outside

As is the case with just about every other kind of cleaning, when you're about to tackle the cleaning of a car you want to take a top-down approach. This is, in part, because just like with everything else, if you clean the bottom first, then all the dirty, soapy water will drip down on the clean parts when you get to the top. But with cars, there's another reason: the dirtiest part of the vehicle is the lower quarter, because the tires kick up dirt, grime, and road tar. And when you're cleaning that stuff off, it gets onto your cleaning rag or mitt . . . then that dirt will stay on the mitt and scratch the car's finish! And we do not want that! Not at all!

The first step when you're washing the car should be to give the entire thing a thorough rinsing with a hose; this will help to dislodge a lot of the dirt and (if it's winter in a cold climate) salt that may be clinging to the car. That hosing down will help to cut down on the amount of time you'll spend cleaning, and also on the potential for getting grit on the mitt that can scratch the car. No grit on the mitt! There's a nice little chant for you to remember. Also, while you're hosing, be sure to get up under the wheel well—a metric ton of road grime has probably collected under there, and if it's left there it can cause rust or body rot. And we do not want that! Not at all!

Right, then once you've hosed your car down, it's time to get washing. Here are the things you'll want to do this:

- A large bucket
- Lukewarm water
- Car wash soap
- Turtle Wax Bug and Tar Remover
- A synthetic chamois
- A shady area
- A cool car *

*I don't mean "cool" in the sense of being popular in high school. I mean, like, *temperature* cool. The reason for this is that if the car is hot, either from just having been shut off or from being out in the baking sun, the suds will dry before you've had a chance to rinse off the cleaning solution, and that can harm the finish of the car. Speaking of the finish of your car! Did you notice how I specified "*car wash* soap" in the list of stuff you need? Take note of that—it's really common to use dish soap to wash a car, and it's not *terrible* to do so, but it will strip the wax off the paint. So if you want to make your wax last longer, which I promise you do, go on and splurge on car wash soap and leave the Palmolive for your best chafing dish. There are a number of car wash soap options out there—Eagle One Easi-Dri Car Wash is one that works well and doesn't leave water spots. But also if you have a car freak in the family or in your circle of friends, you should absolutely ask him or her for product recommendations; you might find that they volunteer to come show you all their cleaning methods! Car people are a very special breed.

For drying the car, a synthetic chamois is a great choice because it's gentle on clear-coat finishes; it will also save you from having to do a ton of extra laundry. To dry, work from the top down, pushing the water off the vehicle, and wring the chamois out regularly. Synthetic chamois can be found in any place that sells automotive products; some brands to look for are Zymol, Detailer's Choice, and my favorite (entirely based on the name), the Absorber. I just love that name! THE ABSORBER. It sounds like an X-Men character. (Is it an X-Men character?)

Now, the next part will make a lot more sense to you: starting with the roof, you'll work in sections, sudsing then rinsing before moving onto the next part. Working on sections will help to ensure that the soap doesn't dry before you've had a chance to rinse it off. Start with the roof, then do the windshield and the rear window. Next up will be the hood, side windows, and trunk.

Once those are cleaned, it's time to focus on the more troublesome parts of the car: when you're cleaning the front end, you'll want to pay special attention to any bugs that may have decided to end it all and chose your vehicle as the perfect place on which to do so. One, they're unsightly; two, bugs are acidic, and that acid can eat through the clear-coat finish on a car, which will cause permanent damage if left untreated. Once you've relieved yourself of bug detail, you'll move along and clean the rear end and sides of the car. The last step in the washing process is to clean the wheels, making sure to get in every nook and cranny and rinsing each wheel with your hose before moving on to the next one.

Now that your car is washed and rinsed and probably looking a million times lovelier than it did when you started, it's time to walk around and admire your work! And also to do a spot check for any residual gunk that you may not have gotten the first time around. If you find any particularly stubborn spots—generally bugs or tar stains—go ahead and hit those with that Turtle Wax Bug and Tar Remover thingy I told you to get. You'll want that. It's not expensive—about six or so bucks?—and it will last you a good long time. So it's well worth having on hand, since repairing the damage to the car's finish that bug corpses will cause will cost you far more than six bucks. You'll spray it on the blemished areas, allow it to penetrate for a minute, and then wipe it away with a clean rag. Then you can buff the area with a soft cloth. If you find that the product is leaving an oily residue, you can go over it with your wash water.

So there are your basics. Probably nothing too earth-shattering there, but now comes the fun part—all the little things that most people don't think of doing but that make all the difference, not just cosmetically but also in terms of the life span of your car. Okay, so! Open all the car doors and the trunk lid so you can wipe down all the doorjambs. Wiping them will dry them off—they definitely have water on them from that massive washing you just did of the exterior!—and will also get them clean. Which is a great thing to do for two reasons: (1) if you think about it, the doorjambs are one of the first things a person sees when they open the car door, so it will create a good impression, and (2) doing so will help to stave off body rot caused by excess moisture.

The very, very, very last thing to do by way of ensuring that no water is hanging around the car just waiting to cause a problem—and I swear this is SO fun—is to get behind the wheel and haul ass around the block, SAFELY, OF COURSE. Haul safely, please! What this does, in addition to just *being awesome*, is that it helps dry the car and drain the car's water channels. That tip comes to me by way of a friend's father, who was a great lover of cars and possessed a fantastic amount of knowledge about their care and keeping. He passed away while I was writing this book, but somewhere up in the great Camaro in the sky, I know he's happy I've shared that with you.

Washing the Car, Part II: The Inside

When it comes to getting the interior of the car clean, it's best to take things in chunks.

Mats and Flooring

The first thing to do by way of cleaning your car mats is to take them out of the car. Then shake-shake-shake-shake-shake. That will help to dislodge a lot of the dirt and grit and such that's trapped in them.

If you have rubber mats, come this way; the rest of you, with the fancy carpeted-type mats, should hang tight for a sec. Rubber mats can be cleaned with water and a small amount of an all-purpose cleaner or soap. If they're very filthy, use a stiff-bristled cleaning brush—here, even a nail brush would work—to scrub the mats and lift off all the dirt. Then rinse them thoroughly using a hose—the force of the water will get off any remaining dirt. If you want to get really fancy about things, as a last step you can apply what's called a "rubber dressing," which will shine the mats back up to their original state. BUT (that's a big but, you see?!) you need to be very careful with these products because if you use the wrong thing, or the right thing improperly, it can cause slipping, which is a bad, bad trait in a car floor mat. So proceed with caution, be sure to ask a salesperson if the product is safe for mats, and follow the manufacturer's instructions to the letter.

Now, then, where are my carpeted car-mat people? Oh, there you are! Okay, you're up now: once your mats are out of the car, you're going to do three things to them in this order: beat, brush, vacuum. I really wish there was a synonym for *vacuum* that started with a *B* to make that more jaunty, but alas, the world is an imperfect place. First up comes the beating, and it's just what it sounds like: you're going to beat the heck out of the backside of the mat, which will dislodge a lot of the trapped dirt and sand and McDonald's french fries. Next up you'll brush the mat out with a stiff-bristled brush, which will help to get out any debris that wasn't completely eliminated by the beating that poor mat just took. The last step will be to vacuum the mat, which will help to restore the nap. Speaking of the nap: when you're in the brushing stage, don't brush too hard—doing so can damage the fibers and ruin the good looks of your mats. And we want you to have handsome mats, so, you know . . . be gentle.

If the mats are really grimy or have spots, you can use a

foaming rug cleaner on them. Just be sure to let them dry thoroughly before you put them back in the car so you don't end up with a mildew problem. Using a clean, dry towel to dry the mats after you've applied the carpet cleaner will help speed that process up.

Fabric Upholstery

When it comes to cleaning dingy-looking fabric upholstery, a good vacuuming can go a long, long way. A handheld vac will be your best friend; it will make the car interior look as gorgeous as you do. If the upholstery is stained, try spot cleaning it with club soda and a white rag. The white rag will allow you to see how much of any given stain you're removing—or *not* removing. If club soda isn't taking out the stains, try using a foam upholstery/rug-cleaning product, which you'll spray on according to the package instructions and blot up with a rag. You do want to be sure to blot at the stain rather than rub at it, which can grind it further into the material.

When you're on the go, a Wet-Nap or baby wipe is a great option for dealing with coffee spills and the like. It's not a bad idea to stash a small package of them somewhere handy.

Leather Upholstery

Leather interiors tend to be a bit easier to keep clean, though they still require some care. If you've got a dark leather interior, you can clean your seats and trim with saddle soap. Apply it in a circular motion with a soft cloth. The saddle soap will clean, condition, soften, and help to protect the leather.

Bonus: you can also use it on your favorite leather boots or handbag!

A lighter leather interior will show grime much more so than a darker leather, so before you use your saddle soap on it, dilute a good dish soap like Palmolive with warm water and use a washcloth or soft rag to give it a little bath. That will help to clean any discoloration caused by dirt and other pollutants. Just be sure to wring the cloth out well—you don't want to saturate the seats with water! Once the seats are looking noticeably cleaner (and they will!), go on and use the saddle soap to condition and protect the leather.

If you find yourself with a grease stain on your leather seats, you can use cornstarch, cornmeal, talcum powder or ground-up chalk to help suck the stain out of the hide. If the stain persists, try using the dish soap and saddle soap technique to get at the last of it.

Seat Belts

Seat belts are filthy. Just . . . take a moment to think about how often your hands touch a seat belt. Right, they're disgusting! But they're super important, and I hope you wear one every time you get into a car because apparently now I'm your nagging mother.

Because seat belts are so important, you need to be mindful of what you're putting on them so that the integrity of the material isn't compromised in any way. SERIOUSLY. DON'T MUCK ABOUT WITH YOUR SEAT BELTS! A mild detergent is the best bet when it comes to getting that belt cleaned up. The dish soap you were using on your leather seats would be a great option. And just like with the upholstery, you want to use only a small amount of water. This is another place where a damp washcloth will be a good choice.

Dashboard and Panels

While there are a lot—a lot a lot a lot—of products out there that bill themselves as dashboard cleaners, the best thing to use on your dash is just a plain old damp rag (if there's stubborn grime, a bit of dish soap will help greatly). Mostly because it's cheap and easy and it works. But also because many of those so-called dashboard cleaning products contain alcohol or ammonia, both of which can cause the dashboard to crack. Which is waaaay not good! The other thing is this: while it may make you happy in the immediate aftermath of cleaning, a shiny-looking dashboard can create glare for the driver, and I don't think I need to tell you why that's not at all a thing anyone wants. Fortunately, you're all wearing your seat belts.

When it comes to getting the panels clean, give 'em a wipe down and then go over them with a round bristle brush or even a paint brush to get out dust and crumbs that may be stuck in control buttons or air vents. Oooh, or a toothbrush! A toothbrush is a great thing for dust and crumb issues in an automobile.

Headlining

Headlining is a fancy term for the interior roof of the car. It's also a lot easier to say than "the interior roof of the car," so we'll hang on to it, yes? Yes!

The good news about the headlining is that, unless you smoke in your car or there's a stain marring its perfection, you needn't clean it all that often. Maybe once a year? The reason you do want to clean it is that over time grime and germs—yes, germs! What, you never sneeze in your car??—can collect on it. You want to take the same approach to cleaning the headlining as you would with fabric upholstery—use an upholstery cleaning product or a diluted dish or laundry detergent and a soft rag that you've dipped in your cleaning solution and wrung out.

Washing the Car, Part III: Getting the McDonald's French Fry Smell Out of the Minivan

Probably the most common car-related questions I get are about smells. So as a general primer here are a few things you can try out if your car stinks. The first thing is our old pal white vinegar: apply some on a clean rag and wipe down all the surfaces, including any upholstery. You don't want a soggy rag, because you don't want to saturate anything with the vinegar. A dampened vinegar rag is what you're going for. The vinegar smell will dissipate and take with it any lingering odors.

If the smell is very strong or very persistent or both, you'll want to use an odor-absorbing product. Two that I like and that people I've recommended them to have sworn by are the Innofresh Auto Odor Eliminator (say that five times fast!) or the Bad Air Sponge. What you *don't* want is an odor-masking product like those rearview mirror trees. You want to remove odors and then add a new, pleasant odor back in if you choose. But just trying to cover up a smell will ultimately result in a McDonald's-french-fry-*and*-pine-tree-smelling car. Which no one wants. Well. Maybe someone wants that, but we don't want to ride in his car, now do we?

Last, don't rule out the power of an open window when it comes to airing out a car—safety and weather permitting, of course! Which brings me to the fun (FUN FUN FUN!) portion of our car-cleaning discussion: DISASTER STORIES! Man, I love a disaster story so much, you guys.

Rainstorms Are Jerks

Jolie, I have a crisis. I accidentally left the sunroof in my car open the other night, which, of course, happened to be the night of a particularly epic thunderstorm. Everything in my car was soaked, which made for a particularly uncomfortable morning commute the next day. It's more or less dried out now, but it reeks. Seriously, it smells so awful, and now I don't want to have any passengers in my car, out of total embarrassment. How do I fix this?

This is such an easy thing to have happen and fortunately there's an easy fix to any lingering smells. Before I get into that, though, it's important that if your car does flood in any way that you check it for mold and mildew once it's dried out. Hopefully there won't be any, but if there is you can kill it with some white vinegar, applied in the way you would to remove smells. It will kill the mold without harming any of the vehicle's interior.

If you don't have mold but do have a smell problem, you can do what this lovely lady did and get your hands on a Bad Air Sponge. They are these super weird things that are sort of gel-like? I dunno, they're totally bizarre, but they totally work. This gal put one under the passenger seat of her stanky car, and a day after our e-mail exchange I got this message from her, which just makes me giggle so much: *I went out and got one yesterday, and holy crap, it is life-changing. Thank you so much for the rec!*

So there you have it! The Bad Air Sponge, life-changing tub of weird goo.

Trees Are Jerks

Ever since I moved into my current apartment a year-ish
ago, I've had to park under a large pine tree that sheds its
needles all over my car. Worse than that is the sap that it
drips throughout the spring and summer. Half of my poor
car was covered in it last year, and since I am decidedly not
a person who loves to clean, it is still on there today. Any
ideas for getting old sap off a car?

Sure thing—that Turtle Wax Bug and Tar Remover stuff
that we talked about during the Cleaning the Exterior portion of the lesson is what you want here. You'll use it like a
spot remover—dab it on the sap, let it sit for a couple of minutes, and then rub it off using a soft cloth. (It may take a little
elbow grease to get it up.) The product is meant to be used
after you've washed the car, but if you notice a slightly oily
residue after usage, you might want to spot treat the sap and
then wash the car. Up to you, really.

Champagne Is a Jerk

So. I bought a bottle of champagne one morning to make
mimosas with a friend. Yummy, right? Well, we ended up
going somewhere and not drinking the champagne and I
had to go to work. I took the bottle with me, drove to work,
left it in my parked car for six hours in the blazing summer
sun, and came back to a car positively splattered with
champagne. Apparently, when it gets hot enough, the cork
will PROJECTILE SHOOT out of the bottle, spewing alco-
hol all over the interior of my car. Jolie, it was everywhere.
I cleaned it up, except for the roof (headlining?). There is
still a large amount of champagne staining there. And it's
been, uh, a few months. Is there any hope?? Help!

The headlining, yes! I love it when you all use your words! Also I love it when I can tell you that there is indeed hope! Especially because it's champagne and not, like, a dark beer that exploded all over the car. Because it's an old stain, you'll want to skip the club soda and go straight to a foaming upholstery cleaner for this job. If it were a fresh stain, I would tell you to get a white cloth and some club soda and let those simple things work their magic. But because you let it sit— and you knew this was coming: don't let stains sit!!! You're breaking my little heart!!! It's a clean break, but still—you're going to need the chemical power of an upholstery cleaner.

Your Boyfriend Is a Jerk

Recently, my boyfriend and I went on a vacation to Martha's Vineyard that turned out to be a terrible trip. (Long story!) We took our bikes, and in the mad rush to get our bags and bikes out of the car, the wheels back on the bikes, and ourselves on the shuttle to the ferry before the ferry left, a bike-grease handprint got on the leather seat of his car. That handprint is probably mine. He's being kind of a jerk about it, which is another deal, but I would genuinely like to correct the mistake. He's pretty attached to the damn car, and the seats are a light gray leather. I am frequently covered in bike grease and find it insidious. What's the best way to get it off? Thank you!

Every time I revisit this question I become furious all over again on behalf of this poor girl. I'm just so mad at the thought of this guy being such a jerk—accidents happen and there's almost always a way to right the wrong when it comes to messes, so making someone feel terrible is a waste of time and negative energy. There's the best piece of advice you'll read here—don't be a jerk in the face of an accident!

Even though this jerk doesn't deserve to have his car cleaned, there's actually a really easy way to get bike grease stains out of leather (and fabric, too!). It sounds kind of strange, but WD-40 is the thing for bike grease stains. I know! Delightful and weird! And actually, WD-40 takes a TON of stains out of things—you should check out their website for the two thousand plus uses that product has.

To use it, you'll spray the stain and let the product sit for fifteen to thirty minutes before wiping it away with a damp sponge with a small bit of dish soap on it to remove any residue. Once you're done, please fetch the boyfriend and GLOAT. The gloating is the best and most important part.

CHAPTER 8

The Things You Really Can't Ask Martha (or Mom, for That Matter!)

We've made it all this way and I know what you're thinking. "This lady is freaking nuts. Also, when do we get the part about barfing in a handbag?"

Well, we're here! We are going to talk about barfing in handbags! And all sorts of other gory tales of messes made. These are the best of the best, or more accurately, the worst of the worst, of the questions people have asked me in my capacity as a Clean Person. Okay, but enough of me telling you about all the great questions I've fielded in my travels, how's about I show you some? I'll ease you in gently, but seriously, BRACE YOURSELVES. Things are about to get really, really real up in this book!

Oh man, you're about to have *so much fun*. I'm kind of jealous.

No Laffing Taffing Matter, or How to Get Goo Out of Your Pocket

Last week I put a Laffy Taffy wrapper in the pocket of my favorite trousers and apparently there was still some Laffy Taffy on that wrapper. How do I get the goo out of my pocket?! Even though I wash everything cold, I worry that washing it could compound the problem, and I would hate to spread green goo to other parts of my awesome pants and/or other items of clothing.

Get an ice cube and a knife. (I wish I could start off every answer with "Get an ice cube and a knife.") What you're going to do is similar to the method we went over when we talked about getting melted plastic up off things in chapter 2. Just like with the plastic (and this goes for wax as well) removal, you'll hold the ice cube on the goo until it hardens, at which point you'll take the knife and very carefully scrape it up off the pants. If the ice cube is too unwieldy for you, you can also just freeze the pants in their entirety before getting after the taffy goo with your knife. Like, put the pants in your freezer. If you live with other people, you'll also probably want to tell them what you're up to before they're all, "Jesus, Mary, and Joseph! Belinda, why are your pants in the freezer?!"

Once that's done, if there's staining, go ahead and spot treat the area and relaunder as usual. And for the love of Pete, check your pockets before you do your laundry!

Lube-stained Sheets, Sure

I found what I suspect is a lube stain on my lovely cotton sheets! If it is lube, it's water-based, so I feel like the stain should just come out in the laundry. Or do I need to

pretreat it? I love this sheet—please help me save it! Also, I
live in Israel, which is like the first-and-a-half world, so I
don't have access to all the same cleaning supplies—like
liquid detergent.

If the lube is water-based then it should come out in the
wash without needing much more than detergent; with that
said, it's certainly still a good idea to apply a spot treatment.
Since you mentioned that you don't have access to a wide
variety of cleaning supplies, liquid dish soap or laundry detergent can serve that function; if you only have powdered
detergent, you can mix it with a small amount of water to
form a paste that can be applied to the stain.

When it comes to silicone-based lubes, things get much,
much more tricky, and so that's a thing you may want to take
into consideration when making lube purchasing decisions.
Along those same lines, I've heard that Astroglide, which is
a water-based lube, has caused sheet staining—so there's no
guarantee that going with a water-based lube will leave you
without a staining problem.

Back to those silicone-based lubes: apparently STP Fuel
Injector & Carburetor Treatment works as a spot treatment
for those sorts of stains. I don't even want to tell you how I
discovered that tip because I like you too much to burden
you with knowledge of the dark, dark places this job often
takes me.

Since we're on the subject of sheet stains—and, oh, you
can bet your bottom dollar there are waaaay more sheet stain
questions a'comin'—how about a brief primer on what to do
about grease stains? I'm talking about the kind of stains that
can be left behind from a heavy night cream or cuticle cream,
or just from rolling around in some olive oil in bed. Because
who among us hasn't done *that*?

Remember back when we talked about cleaning your kitchen, I told you that ammonia is aces on grease? Well, since lotion is just grease for your body, ammonia will work on it, too! I know, it seems sort of wrong, but seriously adding a half to full cup of ammonia to your wash will help eliminate grease stains. Other good options include Lestoil, Pine-Sol, or white vinegar; the latter won't do quite the job of the others, but it will help and is a more eco-friendly option. Applying a solvent-based stain treatment like Shout to the stained areas before washing will also help.

Shit Happens. Hopefully Not on Your Sheets, but If It Does . . .

Men are disgusting. I'd get rid of mine, but I happen to love him. But we do have a problem with my gorgeous bedding and skid marks.

Before you vomit in your mouth, please let me preface that the dude and I have talked about it and come up with a solution for preventing marks from occurring on my white six-hundred-thread-count sheets. He was extremely embarrassed about it and has taken precautions (wet wipes in the bathroom, presex) so it doesn't occur. Most days.

While the solution works, occasionally we crazy kids give in to our baser urges and don't stop for the tingle-killer known as, "Hold on, baby, I need to wipe my ass." When we do the deed without the prewipe session, he usually leaves skids. Or he farts really hard in his sleep and somehow skids occur in the middle of the night. I'm not really sure what's happening while I sleep, but the morning after lurid, nonwiped sex, I usually wake him by lovingly pointing at the area on the sheets with a look of horror on my face.

So my question is, aside from having sex with boxers on, what products could we use to get the skids out of my sheets after the dirty deed? I'd rather not bleach them since I think it will take the sateen finish away. Should I be using something special to get rid of the germs, or does OxiClean wash away my sins along with the skids?

As gross as they are, fecal stains are actually, by the grace of God, fairly easy to manage. But before we get into how to clean up the poop stains, let's detour a bit because the nature of the question has me a little concerned.

Since this is a thing that's happening regularly and is not a common thing for most people to experience, I think your fella should check in with his doctor about what's going on 'round back. There is a thing, and I'm so sorry to have to introduce you to this term, called fecal incontinence, and that might be what's happening with him. It can be caused by a number of things, such as muscle damage to the sphincter or even constipation, some of which are no big deal but some of which may be signs of serious health issues. Either way, best to see a doctor to ensure that nothing is wrong or get treatment if something is off. Treatments, by the way, can range from surgery to medicine to anal kegels. I KNOW! That tickles me pink! Kegels: also for dudes!

Okay, but back to the question at hand—absolutely, Oxi-Clean will help you a lot, though you will want to spot treat the area with it first, and then add a bit more to the wash. Just adding it to the wash without spot treating won't be enough. You can use powdered Oxi mixed with water for this purpose, or you can grab one of their stain-pretreating products; I've had great luck with the OxiClean Max Force Gel Stick. Another product to mention is Borax; it'll give stains a

pretty good run for their money, but it's also gentle enough
that it's commonly recommended for baby laundering. Wait,
no, not *baby* laundering—don't launder your babies! I mean,
you know . . . baby *clothes* laundering. And also, you know
who poops a lot, like, all over the place? Babies. So Borax will
treat you, and your precious sheets, right given what you're
dealing with.

Finally, you mentioned bleach: I don't love bleach for bed
linens because it doesn't play nicely with protein stains, and
our bedclothes are generally full up on protein stains (sweat,
sexual fluids, and the like).

By Comparison, Pee Stains on Mattresses Seem Positively Charming. (No, They Don't.)

*I dated a guy who peed on my mattress. Three times.
He was very, very drunk each time, which I know is no
excuse.*

*Anyway, now we're broken up and I have my mattress in
my new apartment (I couldn't afford to buy a new one). Each
time he peed, I did what my mom used to do with cat pee and
that was to sop up as much mess with paper towels and then
put cornstarch on it to soak up the rest. Then I vacuumed up
the cornstarch once it was dry and did some extra cleaning
with Resolve. I think that did a lot to clean things as the mattress doesn't smell like pee.*

*But there are stains. Telling outlines of where the pee
happened. It just grosses me out every time I take off my
mattress pad to clean it. And what if I someday have a man
friend over and we happen to change the sheets together? I
don't want it to look like I peed the bed, nor do I want to
explain that I dated a man who peed the bed and then had
me clean up his mess (three times!).*

So my question is: how do I get rid of the stain?

Well, look, you got rid of him, didn't you? AND you knew how to get the smells out! So don't be so hard on yourself. I think we've all landed a pisser at one point or another.

Mattress stains are definitely tricky, because you don't want to saturate a mattress and generally when dealing with stains, the power of forced water through the soiled area is a huge boon. With forced water out the window, we're going to have to go with a spot treatment—and here's where things get really fun: products designed for cleaning stains and smells associated with pet accidents are the answer. I know, it seems so obvious when it's laid out there on paper for you, but I needed to be told by *Good Housekeeping*, so don't go feeling bad or anything.

There are a ton of these sorts of products out there, but if you're looking for a really good one, try Bissell's Pet Stain and Odor Remover. You'll use the product as directed, being careful not to go overboard on the spraying so you don't end up saturating the mattress any more than necessary, then blot up the solution with a clean white towel before allowing it to air-dry. You could also turn a fan or hair dryer on it to speed the process along.

Semen Stains, Because Someone Had to Ask

But what about getting the cum stains out of sheets?

Look, let's not mince around and stand on ceremony about how proper we are. We're all out there doing sex to other people, or doing sex to ourselves, and things get leaky as a result.

When we discussed stains I *may* have hollered at you a bit about how you must (must! Must, must, must!) get to stains as soon as possible. However, your sexual stains—and

isn't that such a polite term I've cooked up for us to use here?—
are the one thing that you get a pass on. And here's why: I
want you to enjoy your sex life. Isn't that so nice of me?!

When you are ready to get up out of those sheets that you
just tumbled around in, you'll need to treat the soiled area(s)
with something that will attack protein stains. This means
that you *do not* want to use bleach when laundering any bed
linens that may have seminal fluid on them, as the bleach
will render those areas yellow and therefore noticeably, um,
sperm-stained. Once you've spot treated the stains, go on
and wash the bedding as you normally would.

Those Sex Toys Aren't Going to Clean Themselves, Sweet Cheeks

*How does one clean her sex toys—silicone, glass, and every-
thing in between? I have a friend who wants to know. And
this friend really loves her toys.*

Well, who doesn't love her toys?! I'm, however, a little concerned here that someone who sounds like she has an impres-
sive collection of toys might not know how to clean them,
because that suggests that they've never *been* cleaned, and
let's move on before I have to complete that thought.

Because sex toys come in so many varieties, there's no one
absolute way to clean them—you need to know what material type you have and proceed accordingly. This is information that you should either ask about when you're buying the
piece, or look for on the packaging if you're too embarrassed
to speak to a human about the ten-inch dildo you just treated
yourself to. (Related: good for you!)

Before getting into the specifics of cleaning silicone versus glass, a few general tips to consider:

- Don't use anything to clean your sex toys that you wouldn't put in your body. That means that things like rubbing alcohol, bleach, all-purpose cleaner, etc., are out when it comes to giving your toys a bath.
- Make sure the toys are completely dry before storing them.
- If your toy has a motor that isn't waterproof, don't ever submerge it in water. Wipe it down with a soapy cloth instead to avoid flooding the motor.
- You can run a load of (unmotorized) dildos through the dishwasher! Isn't that a hilarious mental image to conjure up?? Put them in the top rack, and don't use dishwashing soap—the combination of the hot water and steam will get them sufficiently clean.
- Hard plastic, elastomer, TPR, and jelly rubber are all porous, which means you *must* use a condom if you are going to share toys made of those materials with a partner.
- Use a condom for easy cleanup or when in doubt.
- And finally: toy cleaner, which can be found at most stores where toys are sold, is great for when you *just can't* get out of bed.

With those general thoughts out of the way, here's the 411 on cleaning your toys, broken down by material type:

Material Type	What to Use	What Not to Use	Miscellany
Silicone (no motor)	• Soap and water • Boiling water	Anything you wouldn't put in your body, e.g., rubbing alcohol, bleach, all-purpose cleaner, etc.	Boil for eight to ten minutes to disinfect before the first use and/or between uses
Silicone (with motor)	Soap and water	Anything you wouldn't put in your body, e.g., rubbing alcohol, bleach, all-purpose cleaner, etc.	Don't submerge in water, use a soapy cloth to wipe clean
Glass	Soap and water	• Excess heat • Anything you wouldn't put in your body, e.g., rubbing alcohol, bleach, all-purpose cleaner, etc.	Extreme heat can cause the glass to shatter, just like with a drinking glass
Pyrex	• Soap and water • Boiling water	Anything you wouldn't put in your body, e.g., rubbing alcohol, bleach, all-purpose cleaner, etc.	Boil for eight to ten minutes to disinfect before the first use and/or between uses
Stainless Steel (no motor)	• Soap and water • Boiling water	Anything you wouldn't put in your body, e.g., rubbing alcohol, bleach, all-purpose cleaner, etc.	Boil for eight to ten minutes to disinfect before the first use and/or between uses
Stainless Steel (with motor)	Soap and water	Anything you wouldn't put in your body, e.g., rubbing alcohol, bleach, all-purpose cleaner, etc.	Don't submerge in water, use a soapy cloth to wipe clean
Hard Plastic	Soap and water	Anything you wouldn't put in your body, e.g., rubbing alcohol, bleach, all-purpose cleaner, etc.	N/A

Elastomer and TPR	Soap and water	Anything you wouldn't put in your body, e.g., rubbing alcohol, bleach, all-purpose cleaner, etc.	N/A
Wood	Soap and water	Anything you wouldn't put in your body, e.g., rubbing alcohol, bleach, all-purpose cleaner, etc.	N/A
Stone	• Soap and water • Boiling water	• Acidic products (vinegar, lemon juice) • Anything you wouldn't put in your body, e.g., rubbing alcohol, bleach, all-purpose cleaner, etc.	Boil for eight to ten minutes to disinfect before the first use and/or between uses
Jelly Rubber	Soap and water	Anything you wouldn't put in your body, e.g., rubbing alcohol, bleach, all-purpose cleaner, etc.	N/A
CyberSkin	Damp cloth	• Excessive amounts of soap • Anything you wouldn't put in your body, e.g., rubbing alcohol, bleach, all-purpose cleaner, etc.	CyberSkin is the material used in Fleshlights. It's made of mineral oil, which means that it should be washed with as little soap as possible, if you must use soap at all. Further instructions on the care of CyberSkin can be found on the Fleshlight website.

Harness Care—and Stop Acting So Shocked!

I have this fabulous, sexy leather strap-on harness. Or, I should say, my girlfriend has it. I have orgasms. Sometimes it stays pretty clean and we can, as recommended by the store where we bought it and its packaging, just wipe it down with a damp cloth. However, sometimes it gets some pretty heavy contact and the damp-cloth method is just not cutting it. Plus, germs!

Since we don't want to get the leather too wet due to concerns about stretching and the like, our options seem to be leather cleaner and leather oil. Neither of which disinfect, methinks, nor do they feel especially safe to rub all around my ladyparts. Which, of course, is the fun.

Also, it has nice rivets and snaps to hold the ring that holds the dildo in place. Little crevices of metal on leather. It's driving me so nuts about how hard/weird it is to clean that it's affecting the frequency with which we use it! Also it's bothering me that I can't find this answer anywhere. Are there seriously no lesbians on the Internet who are meticulous about cleaning their things? 'Tis a puzzlement.

A puzzlement indeed! How is this a thing that the Internet has not yet addressed? Ah well, it just gives me an excuse to do some original reporting, and I'm never going to turn down that sort of opportunity.

Because I live in lower Manhattan, it's easy enough for me to scamper over to a Chelsea leather shop and find some experts on cleaning leather gear used in and around sexual acts. So that's what I did. I had an enjoyable and highly informative chat that yielded the following suggestions and tips:

1. For day-to-day cleaning, use baby wipes. The low moisture content will keep the leather from getting water

damage but will provide just enough by way of suds to clean off any fluids left behind after a romp between the sheets.

2. For maintenance, you can use saddle soap and/or mink oil. Do this before you store it away, which will allow the products to set into the leather—that way they won't end up on your parts.

3. For deep cleaning, you can take the items to the dry cleaner. Yes, really. Quoth the fellow with whom I spoke, "They've seen everything; they're used to it."

Now, then, a quick note about that last statement: it's true that dry cleaners have likely seen most everything. But still remember to be respectful of them and their place of business and wipe off as much mess as you can before you bring the harness in for cleaning.

Diva Cake

How do I clean my DivaCup? I mean, it's totally clean; I wash it every time I empty it, and I boil it to sanitize it after. But it's . . . yellowing. Is that just what silicone does, and I have to live with it? I CAN live with it, but . . . maybe I should add some vinegar when I boil it!

Oh no, don't use vinegar on your DivaCup!

First things first: the DivaCup website has super great, detailed instructions that you should check out. With that said, the basics of cleaning a silicone menstrual cup are pretty similar to those for sex toys: you want to wash it using mild soap and water. You can also boil the Cup for five to ten minutes. You'll want the water to be rolling along at a good clip, and you do not want to use a lid once the Cup is in the pot. Pretty simple!

Do NOT use vinegar, hydrogen peroxide, tea tree oil, scented soap, oil-based soaps (castile, peppermint, lavender, etc.), dish soap, antibacterial soap, hand sanitizer, moistened wipes, rubbing alcohol, or bleach.

If your DivaCup becomes discolored, try boiling it. If that doesn't work, as is your case, it may just be that the silicone has been compromised and you can choose whether it bothers you enough to purchase a new one. The Diva people offer something called DivaWash that may be the ticket to preventing discoloration in the first place, but I'm naturally suspicious of single-use products marketed by companies that have a vested interest in selling you on extras to bank coin.

One final note on menstrual cups: the soft ones, as opposed to the silicone ones like the DivaCup, can be worn during sex. We covered the cleaning of bloodstains pretty extensively back when we talked about laundry, but I think it's worth mentioning that if you're a period sex aficionado— and good for you if you are!—you might want to try it out while wearing a soft cup to cut down the amount of mess making that particular practice can cause.

Stoners Can Be Clean People Too, You Know

I have a very San Francisco Clean Person question for you—actually on behalf of my attractive lady friend (ha cha cha). We are wondering: what's the best way to clean a bong? And also, if it is not the same, what's the most environmentally sound method?

I love it when dudes try to impress their ladies with a sparkling clean bong. Also the answer to this one is so fun: denture tablets or Alka-Seltzer. Drop a tablet in, fill with warm water, let the fizzing take care of the cleaning, and then rinse. BOOM. A clean bong.

For smaller glass pipes, you can place the piece into a large bowl and use the same technique. If you don't have denture tablets or Alka-Seltzer handy, you really should change that, or you can cover the pipe with baking soda and fill the bowl halfway up with white vinegar. Maybe a little less than halfway. Because, you know, there's going to be a COOL-ASS VOLCANO! And by all means, do feel free to use that pipe *before* you make the volcano! Because, right? "Whoa." While you're busy whoa ing, let it sit tight for a while (ten, fifteen or so minutes?) so that the volcano can work its magic, then rinse with warm water.

Another similar method is to put your piece in a plastic takeout container or other lidded vessel filled with equal parts rubbing alcohol and warm water. Then sprinkle a fairly liberal amount of kosher salt into the mix, lid it up, and shake it like a Polaroid picture. Once that's done, let it sit for thirty to sixty minutes, rinse, and hit the innards with a pipe cleaner. The gunk will shimmy right off.

Bong Water on the Carpet

I knocked over my bong—now bong water is all over my carpet, and it STINKS! What do I do??

Oh, how perfectly vile. Bong water is FOUL. I'm surprised they've not yet fashioned a weapon of mass destruction around the putrid stuff.

As you correctly noted, the problem with bong water is less the staining—though it does have that disgusting brown hue to it—and more the stench of it. The best way to clean up spills on carpeting is to use a foaming carpet cleaner (we talked about a bunch of those back in chapter 2); when it comes to spills that also really stink, look for a product that offers odor eliminating. Arm & Hammer makes a good one, and most carpet cleaners marketed for use on pet stains will also work to kill smells.

To help get the smell out of the room, set out a small bowl of white vinegar, which will absorb the smells lurking in the air.

Speaking of Smoking: On the Road with Gross Smoky Smelling Clothes

Scenario: you're traveling and only have, like, two outfits for a weekend, end up in a smoky hotel bar one night, and have to wear an article of clothing (a shirt or something) again the next day, but you're like, in a hotel. How can you best freshen it up?

Though I'm not the biggest fan of odor-masking products, travel is one place where things like Febreze or Zero Odor really shine: both brands offer travel-size spray bottles of their products, which you could throw into a cosmetics bag as a just-in-case precaution. Similarly, if you think ahead, toss a small stack of dryer sheets in your suitcase—they'll help to keep everything smelling fresh and can be rubbed onto any items that are particularly smoky smelling.

If you've got a travel steamer, fill it with a white vinegar and water solution and give your clothes a once-over. The vinegar will help to eliminate the smells; if you can't get ahold of vinegar, steaming with just water will also help.

Can you get your hands on a spray bottle? If so, raid the minibar for a nip of vodka, pour it in the spray bottle, and spritz away—vodka will also kill smoke smells. Yes, really, vodka. I *told* you you were gonna have fun!

The Curious Case of Boy Smell

I recently moved into a house of dudes. There are six of us living in the house, and I am the only girl. I am also the only one who makes any attempt at keeping our space "nice." I say "nice" because if you saw photos of the common areas it would look pretty decent. The problem is the smell. Even when the garbage has been taken away and everything is freshly vacuumed and mopped, a smell lingers. I would say that it is a combination of dirty socks, stale deodorant, beer, and a general layer of dirt/dust.

The floors are wood, so it's not like I can just rip out some carpet. We have fans on 24/7 in the living room, so there's not really an issue of poor air circulation. I just cleaned out the fridge. There is no rotting food in the pantry. We're all smokers but generally keep that constrained to the outdoors. I'm definitely beyond Febreze-able territory here, and I'm wondering if there is a magical way to get rid of this beer/foot/stale smell that permeates the house. I'm kind of assuming it has been ingrained into the floors and walls and that nothing short of a giant Arm & Hammer baking soda box installed in the foyer could do the trick, however, any suggestion is greatly appreciated.

The bad news is that you've contracted an acute case of Boy Smell. The good news is that Boy Smell is very treatable.

The first order of business is to give the common areas a thorough vinegaring, which will go a long way in eliminating the embedded Boy Smell. Here's what you're going to do: round up the roommates and start issuing orders: "LISTEN UP, LADS. TODAY WE ARE DOUCHING THE HOUSE." Say it just like that.

Fill up a couple of big bowls with a white vinegar solution

(equal parts water and vinegar) and give each person a clean
rag. Their instructions are as follows: dip a rag in the solution,
wring it out, and go over every surface with the vinegar solution rag, followed by a wax-on-, wax-off-type motion with a
dry rag. Do be sure to use the *Karate Kid* metaphor. Speak to
them in their language, if you will. Explain to them that they
want to go over the walls, floors, nonupholstered furniture,
etc. I suspect that the upholstered furniture is also harboring
Boy Smell, in which case you can take a page out of the book
our friend with the cigarette smoke-smelling clothes is reading and spritz down the couches and whatnot with a spray
bottle filled with vodka. You can do that while they're doing
the walls so they don't feel like you're slacking off. Also, with
a few people working together, this process should take no
more than thirty minutes. Probably fewer.

Once that's done, you'll want to prevent the smell from
coming back. This is where odor absorbers—not odor mask-
ers like Febreze or air fresheners!—come in. Get a few canis-
ters of the Bad Air Sponge or some activated charcoal odor
absorbers and scatter them around the common areas (you
can sort of tuck them in corners or behind furniture).

And, look, if you can't make them submit for the vinegaring, just put out the Sponges. If you can sneak into their
rooms and hide Sponges under their beds, even better.

The Jizzcliner

*I'm moving in with my boyfriend who wants to bring his
old La-Z-Boy recliner with us to the new place. This is fine
by me except for the fact that the arm of the velour-like fabric is covered in old semen. Like visible stains on the green
fabric. I don't want to bring the old semen with us, so is
there any way to get rid of the stains??*

May I say that you are one seriously permissive girl-friend? I mean, it takes one to know one, but still . . . *wow*. A semen-stained green La-Z-Boy. Congratulations on winning the Best Girlfriend Ever pageant! Love your sash!

The quick and dirty solution is to hit that stain with Oxi-Clean. But you know that by now because the words *protein stain* are now etched onto your brain. Sorry about that! In fairness, I did warn you that this wasn't going to be for the faint of heart.

Because you're dealing with upholstery, you need to be careful not to saturate it with too much water. If you've got powdered Oxi, mix it with a small amount of water, let it dissolve (hot water is best for this), and then with a damp—not soaking, damp—towel, apply the solution to the fabric. Instead of letting it sit, which can cause the fabric to discolor, you want to just blot, blot, blot, blot, blot, gently rubbing at the fabric to pull up the crusted-on splooge.

While you're going about this business, do be sure to sweet-talk the recliner and turn to your boyfriend to inform him that now he's not the only one in the family who's had a romantic interlude with the La-Z-Boy.

Once you've gotten the stain up, let the chair air-dry or turn the hair dryer on it. When the chair is dry, go over it with a vacuum fitted with a brush attachment. That will help to restore the nap back to its former, pre-cum-Dumpster state.

Another option you have is renting a steam cleaner, which you might want to do anyway. Hardware stores, grocery stores—those are the kinds of places you'll find steam-cleaning equipment rentals. Ask the rental folks what kind of cleaning solution they recommend for their machine/what works best for the type of fabric you've got. If they ask what sort of stain you're dealing with and you're too embarrassed to tell them the truth, just keep the protein stains in the family and tell them it's barf.

My Boyfriend Barfed in My Handbag

Please help save my beautiful leather handbag. My boy-friend made it a party casualty. (What, you shouldn't mix tequila and vodka? And champagne? And so much Franzia? And also whiskey shots?) I was able to deal with the stains by scrubbing the bag with just the sudsy bubbles from a bowl of lukewarm water and a sponge. However, now the leather is kind of crunchy and, well, leathery, and it STILL smells like vom. Febreze didn't work, and I'm afraid to use lemon. Please help save my bag!

Oh no, you poor, sweet girl. I'm so upset for you and your handbag! What kind of monster boyfriend commits such horrible crimes against leather goods? I'm going to presume that he's sufficiently humbled and groveling and doing nice things like not complaining when you stick your ice-cold feet on his warm legs when you get into bed at night.

Also, I would like to applaud you for doing just the right thing with sudsy bubbles and getting that vomit out! Look at you go! The two issues you've got to handle, the crunchy feel of the leather and the smell, are easily addressed. You'll need to get two products, and you'll be able to get other use out of them too, so that's great. The first is saddle soap, which will help to soften that leather back up. There are many brands of saddle soap, so you should follow the directions on the package of whichever brand you choose. Saddle soap can also be used on any nonvomit-y bags or leather shoes that you want to shine up a bit.

The other thing I want you to get is a product designed for getting the stink out of running shoes. These generally come in a can and can be found at drug stores, sporting goods stores, online on Amazon, etc. These products are designed to be safe on leather, as many athletic shoes have leather parts, and so they'll eliminate the smell without damaging your handbag. Give the interior of the bag a good blast with it—it may take more than one spray to completely rid the bag of the smell if it's very, very strong, but hang in there and it will eventually go away.

Good grief. Barf in a handbag. I would say I've seen it all, but I know that if I do, the forces of Clean *and* Filthy will band together and deliver unto me cleaning conundrums I wouldn't be able to cook up in my wildest dreams.

Acknowledgments

Unless I want to lose a friend, I have to start by thanking Tyler Coates for clapping me on the shoulder at a holiday party and ordering me to write about cleaning. He was onto something, I think! Thank you, also, to the wonderful editors who have supported my column, "Ask a Clean Person": Edith Zimmerman, Choire Sicha, Tommy Craggs, and Jessica Coen.

This book would not be here if not for the tireless guidance and cheerleading of my wonderful editor Allison Lorentzen and my incredible agent Rachael Dillon Fried.

Mostly, though, I owe the biggest debt of gratitude to all the people who have trusted me with their often gross, often touching, always surprising questions about cleaning and the stories behind the messes.

Index